# An Undivided Heart:

## Lessons from the Kings of Judah

D0126714

# D. Michael Henderson

Michael Henderson is the Executive Director of Heart of Africa, a mission whose purpose is to help our African colleagues fulfill their God-given ministries.

Find out more at:
www.heartofafrica.org

Scripture quotations, unless noted otherwise, are taken from the Holy Bible: New International Version ®. NIV ®. Copyright © 1973, 1978, 1984, by International Bible Society. Used by permission of Zondervan Bible Publishers. All rights reserved. Italics have been added to Scripture quotations for emphasis.

Interior Design: Shawna Lundin/Upward Publishing and Design
Cover Design: Shawna Lundin/Upward Publishing and Design

ISBN: 978-0-9903459-1-6

Rafiki
Books

Rafiki Books
P.O. Box 5, Wilmore, Kentucky 40390
www.rafikibooks.

*These studies are dedicated to my friend Nathan Price,*
*a man with an undivided heart toward God.*

# Table of Contents

# Chronology of the
# Kings of Judah

# Introduction

A grand theme runs through the pages of the Bible like a golden thread: God is seeking a heart-to-heart relationship with the people he created. In Genesis, God reaches out to Adam, to Enoch, to Noah, to Abraham, to Moses. He assures them he wants to have an intimate friendship with them and to show them how to live in harmony with each other and with the world he has created for them. In some cases, they respond and a bond is established. However, all too often, they spurn his appeals and insist on doing things their own way. It is an epic love story, an unfolding drama, filled with pleasant episodes and tragic scenes.

As scripture unfolds, God presents this same invitation to individuals, tribes, and nations: "Come to me. Live in spiritual unity with me. I will be your God. I want you to be my people." At the end of the Bible, in the Book of Revelation, that drama reaches a triumphal climax. The bridegroom receives the bride, the king is crowned among his adoring subjects, and the love story is fulfilled. The friendships that were established on earth are extended into eternity.

One episode in that drama is the friendship of God with David, the shepherd boy who became king. In many ways their interaction is a model of what God intends: God takes the initiative to develop a relationship with this person. David responds to God's initiatives with affection and loyalty. According to the prophet Samuel, he is "a man after God's own heart." David sings psalms to God, loves his law, and seeks to please him in every way. God blesses David with further revelations and the resources he needs to establish an earthly kingdom. It is not, however, a perfect story. It isn't a fairy tale. On some occasions it is marred by David's own poor choices and deliberate transgressions.

The next 600 years of the history of David's family are recorded in the books of I and II Chronicles. Initially, this was one book, so we will simply refer to the whole story as "Chronicles." The parallel history, recorded in I and II Kings, is a corroboration of Chronicles and is supported by the prophecies of Jeremiah, Isaiah, Ezekiel, and Amos. This drama has a cast of millions: not only the individual kings in David's line of succession, but emperors, villains, soldiers by the thousands, the ordinary citizens of the nation of Judah, messengers, prophets, and priests.

The overarching theme is constant: God is seeking a people to love him, to be joined together at the heart with him. He wants an intimate friendship with them as individuals and as a nation. He reveals to them his willingness to make an unbreakable commitment, a covenant, with them, and he wants them to make a life-long heart commitment to him in return. Although the characters and historical settings and sub-plots change, God's purpose never wavers. Through it all, he is faithful to his stated intention, but they must respond in good faith and heart-felt devotion.

There is an intriguing phrase which occurs fourteen times in the books of I and II Kings and I and II Chronicles. It is the standard, the benchmark, the yardstick by which the kings of Judah are measured. It is one key to understanding the entire drama of scripture, the unfolding of the rest of God's redemptive story, the one which began with Adam and ends with the Second Adam, Jesus Christ.

That phrase is "an undivided heart." It is *lebab shalame* in Hebrew. I'm certainly not a Hebrew scholar, as my son Joe is, but I do know how to look up the words in the lexicon. *"Lev/lebab"* is the Hebrew word for "heart." Unlike our English word "heart," which also means a physical organ, *lev* has nothing to do with the physical heart. It is the center of a person's being, the sum total of his or her affections, loyalties, convictions, motivations, attitudes, and feelings.

The word *shalame* is the adjective form of the common Hebrew blessing, *Shalom! Shalame* means "complete," "total," "all together," or (as I prefer to translate it) "undivided." The greeting *Shalom!* is often translated simply as "Peace," but it means far more than that. It means "May God bless you in every area of your life!" or

"I wish you complete well-being!" So, I like to read *lebab shalame* as "an undivided heart."

The most succinct expression of the importance of an "undivided heart" is the word of the prophet to King Asa:

> **"The eyes of the Lord run to and fro throughout the entire earth to show himself strong on behalf of those whose hearts are undivided toward him."**
> II Chronicles 16:9 KJV

The King James Version of the Bible uses the word "perfect" for *shalame* in this passage, but I avoid that term to stay as far away as I can from people who interpret God's desire for his people to be moral perfection. In Jesus' day, the Pharisees claimed "sinless perfection," but he pointed out that their self-righteousness was not the kind of "perfection" God wanted. An undivided, totally devoted, fully committed, completely loyal heart is what God seeks.

In Chronicles, God reveals himself as a loving father who not only wants his children to live well, but to live in communion with him. He is relentless in his search for one thing: their sincere and exclusive affection for him. With his fatherly ability to detect the condition of their hearts, his "eyes run to and fro throughout the entire earth" to find those who will respond to his entreaties. When they respond, he "makes himself strong on their behalf." He gives them peace and prosperity, and he is their God. They enjoy his presence in their temple worship and their quiet meditations. They pay attention to his prophets and messengers. They pursue justice and obey his laws. They observe the ritual of the Passover, in which they remember that God delivered them from bondage in Egypt.

When God's overtures to the people of Israel are spurned, his messengers ignored (or killed), or his laws flouted, he cuts them off. He turns his back on them. He takes away his providing and protecting hand and allows them to suffer the consequences of their own choices.

As an earthly father, I understand God's desire in a small way: Martha and I have two wonderful daughters, Kathryn and Laura. When they grew up, two young men made appointments with us to ask our blessing on their intentions. They each had the same request: "I want to marry your daughter."

Can you imagine our response if either of them had said, "I really like your daughter, and I want to include her among the other women in my life. I like her so much I can probably give her 60%, or maybe even 70%, of my affection and attention. Of course, I can't promise how long I'll feel this way, but I'm willing to give it a try."

Naturally, we would say, "No way!"

Now, of course, that didn't happen. In fact, it pleases us that both of those men love our daughters with "undivided hearts." Because of their whole-hearted commitment to our girls, we are eager to "show ourselves strong on their behalf." We want to make whatever resources we have available to them on the basis of only one quality: not the fact that they are brilliant fellows (which they happen to be), or that they share all our opinions (which they don't), or that they do everything we wish they would. Whatever is appropriate for us to provide for them, we will give. If they ever need any kind of help, we will make any sacrifice to see that they have what they need. We will not only do this willingly and cheerfully; we delight in giving them everything within our power to give.

Our desire is not just that our sons-in-law enjoy physical and material well-being. They have our hearts, and we want theirs, based on their loyalty to our daughters. We want to spend our vacations with them, talk with them on the phone as often as is sensible, laugh, exchange gifts, and "walk with them in the cool of the evening," just as God walked with Adam. We want to have as intimate friendship with them as they will allow.

This same kind of love story is recorded in the Book of Chronicles. God found one fellow whose heart was right: David. He made promises to this shepherd king. He enjoyed David's friendship and revealed to David his "ways." And he made a promise to David that succeeding generations of David's family would rule over the nation of Israel.

The Chronicles drama may be a bit too black-and-white,

too harsh, for the taste of those who prefer a more subtle story line. The plot is like that of an old western movie: the good guys wear white hats, the villain gets shot in the end, and the hero marries the beautiful girl and gets the ranch, too.

The story of Manasseh is typical:

> *"Manasseh was twelve years old when he became king, and he reigned in Jerusalem fifty-five years. He did evil in the eyes of the Lord, following the detestable practices of the nations the Lord had driven out before the Israelites."*
>
> II Chronicles 33:1-2

> *"The Lord spoke to Manasseh and his people, but they paid no attention. So the Lord brought against them the army commanders of the king of Assyria, who took Manasseh prisoner, put a hook in his nose, bound him with bronze shackles and took him to Babylon. In his distress he sought the favor of the Lord his God and humbled himself greatly before the God of this fathers. And when he prayed to him, the Lord was moved by his entreaty and listened to his plea; so he brought him back to Jerusalem and to his kingdom. Then Manasseh knew that the Lord is God."*
>
> II Chronicles 33:10-13

This is the plot line for all those kings who followed David:

1. They can choose to have an undivided heart toward God, as David did, or they can turn away from him and worship false gods.

2. However, if they choose to turn their backs
   on God, he sends a messenger to warn them
   of dire consequences.
3. If they don't listen, he withdraws his blessing
   and protection. Bad things happen, usually
   inflicted by their ungodly neighbors.
4. If they repent, they are restored to fellowship
   with God and to the peace and prosperity he
   grants to his children.

Chronicles records the period during which God's
rivals for the hearts of his people are the religions of
the surrounding empires—the Assyrians, Egyptians,
Babylonians, and the Canaanites. Those cultures had no
comprehension of a God who created the universe and
stands outside it. Rather, they worshipped the creation
itself: the sun, the earth, the moon, the Nile River. Their
religion did not cause them to behave nobly, but to engage
in disgusting practices to appease or influence the forces
of nature: child sacrifices, sexual deviance, worship of
man-made objects which represent the forces of nature,
and flouting the rules for behavior which God had
revealed. So, David's successors had to choose: the God
who reveals or the gods of their powerful neighbors.

The Chronicles story of God's relationship with the
descendents of David sheds light on some important
issues relative to God's relationship with the people he
created. Is this primarily a family issue or a legal one?
Should we visualize our standing with God and define
our relationship to him in terms of father or judge?

Let's go back to our relationship with our sons-in-law. They enjoy both a legal bond and a familial bond with our daughters. They are bound to our daughters by both law and by blood. So, which relationship is primary? Is marriage a legal relationship or a personal commitment? As long as their hearts are right, the family relationship is primary. The law is secondary, really unnecessary in most situations. However, if that bond of loyalty is irreparably broken, then a judge must take control. The impersonal hand of the law will decide their fate, and it won't be pleasant.

Consider a parallel illustration: Aircraft are designed to travel through the air by applying the principles of aerodynamics to overcome the force of gravity. As long as they abide by those principles, the laws of aerodynamics keep them flying. They have the marvelous ability to glide through the air, carrying passengers and freight to distant locations. However, if an aircraft fails to comply with the laws of aerodynamics, the law of gravity takes over and the results are not pleasant. There has never been an incidence of an aircraft defying the laws of gravity outside the principles of aerodynamics.

So it is with people, like us. We were designed to live in heart union with God. As long as that bond is secure, we enjoy God's company and the benefits of membership in his family. If we do or say things that displease him, which always happens in families, he corrects us like a father. If we severely offend him, he severely disciplines us. However, if the heart bond is broken, if we turn our loyalty away from him, the law takes over. The retribution we receive for our wrongdoing is no longer family discipline; it is punishment. We are no longer dealing with God our father; we are dealing with God the judge.

The purpose of this study is first to see the books of I and II Chronicles as a love story between God and his people, specifically David and those of his successors who were kings of Judah. It is not intended to be either a historical handbook or a scholarly examination of the text of those books. Rather, it is an attempt to look at examples from human history which illustrate a spiritual principle.

There is also a motive which aims at the heart of the reader: to establish or solidify the conviction that God is actively seeking to build a friendship with people who will be loyal to him, who have "an undivided heart." This is one slice of the whole fabric of both Old and New Testaments, but consistent throughout. The second part of that thesis is that God desires "to show himself strong" on their behalf. Just as God made his power and provision available to David in order to establish an earthly kingdom, he still is eager to bless his children to build the Kingdom of God. The eyes of the Lord are still running to and fro throughout the entire earth to show himself strong on behalf of those who have an undivided heart toward him.

The ultimate aim is that someone who reads these pages will say, "By God's grace, I will be that person."

# CHAPTER 1

# David: A Man After God's Own Heart

*"Man looks at the outward appearance, but the Lord looks at the heart."*　　　　　　　　I Samuel 16:7b

The biblical portrait of David, the shepherd king, towers over the panorama of the Old Testament like the statue of Colossus stood astride the harbor at Rhodes. His life story dominates the history of God's chosen people, not only because he ushered in the golden age of Israel's history, nor because of his vision to construct the temple in Jerusalem—not even because of his role in the line of Jesus, the Messiah, the "son of David." He was preeminent among the characters of the Old Testament because he was the embodiment, the ideal, the model of what God intended: a man with an undivided heart, an unswerving loyalty to God. This is the central theme of the drama of revelation: that God desires an intimate friendship, first with a person, then with a people.

The writers of scripture dispensed with the creation of the universe and all its inhabitants in just three chapters; in twelve chapters, they recorded the life and times of Abraham, the father of the Jewish nation. But they took sixty-six chapters to tell the life of David and many more to record his psalms, the prophecies concerning his kingdom, and the plight of his successors on the throne of Judah.

When the prophet Samuel was commissioned to find a replacement for King Saul, God gave him the standard for spiritual leadership: he must be "a man after God's own heart." (I Samuel 13:14) As the Lord explained to Samuel:

> *"Man looks at the outward appearance, but the Lord looks at the heart."*                    I Samuel 16:7b

A pure heart is more important to God than any or all other qualities. For that reason above all others, David was chosen to be king (Acts 13:22), and his moniker was forever to be: "A man after God's own heart."

Throughout the Bible, both Old and New Testaments, the critical issue is always the alignment of a person's heart. The "set" of the heart determines every issue of life, like the set of the sail determines the course of a ship. As the writer of Proverbs says,

*"Keep your heart with all diligence, for out of it spring the issues of life."*     Proverbs 4:23 KJV

Throughout the centuries, seekers after God have found insights from the life of David to aid them in their own pilgrimage. Perhaps we, too, can gain some practical guidance for our own spiritual quests. What was it about this man that caused God to bless him above all others and to make an extravagant covenant with him? How did he become "a man after God's own heart?" More importantly, what lessons can we glean from David's life that will help us, too, become people with undivided hearts?

First of all, David played to an audience of one. As the drama of his life played out on the stage of the nation of Israel, he had a vast audience of people watching him: devoted followers, fierce enemies, intimate friends, and harsh critics. He could have focused his performance on any one of those sets of watchers. However, he never took his eyes off the One whose approval he sought.

From an early age, the focus of his affection was Godward. His passion was to know God and to please him. That deep desire framed every experience. When he was tending his father's sheep, his mind was on God. When he lay awake on the mountainside, under the starry heavens, he composed songs of devotion to God. Whenever he faced seemingly impossible obstacles, like lions and bears and giants, he faced them in confidence of God's presence and provision. And, when the time came to pass on his greatness to his son, the one thing he prayed for Solomon was that he would have an undivided heart.

David discovered at an early age the link between an undivided heart toward God and a life of blessing. David never considered that his accomplishments were his own doing. He took it for granted that God was responsible for all the good that happened. When he was able to kill the lion and the bear, he never said, "Look what I did." He always gave credit to God—not because it was his duty, but because he couldn't imagine it any other way. David saw the connection between his devotion to God and the ability to do what God intended.

Whenever he messed up, as in his adultery with Bathsheba and the subsequent cover-up, he acknowledged that the primary offense was against God Himself. Yes, he had violated Bathsheba's honor and sent her husband Uriah to certain death in battle. And, yes, he had broken Israel's code of ethics. But his remorse was addressed first to God. In anguish he prayed:

> *"For I know my transgressions, and my sin is always before me. Against you, you only, have I sinned and done what is evil in your sight."*                          Psalm 51:3-4

When he determined to right the wrong, he did not go first to Bathsheba nor make a public confession to the people of Israel. No, he pled with God to cleanse his heart. (Psalm 51:7-12)

Secondly, David had a fierce zeal for the reputation of God. "Glory" is God's reputation: how people think of him, how people perceive God to be. Human beings cannot see the character of God, the holiness of God, but we can be aware of his glory. We can recognize the reflection of his character through his mighty acts, his revealed Word, and through the lives of the people he has touched. David was able to infer from all God had created and done and said, that God is holy and powerful and just and loving and worthy of our total allegiance.

The positive aspect of David's zeal for God's glory was his passion that everyone, every nation, the whole world would come to acknowledge the beauty and holiness and goodness of God. His heart ached for his own people to bow in reverence before the God he loved. He knew about other nations who worshipped all kinds of inferior "gods," and he agonized over their lost condition.

> *"Among the gods there is none like you, O Lord; no deeds can compare with yours. All the nations you have made will come and worship before you, O Lord; they will bring glory to your name. For you are great and do marvelous deeds; you alone are God."* Psalm 86:8-10

He longed for the day when all the people of the world would bow in reverence for God:

> *"All the ends of the earth will remember and turn to the Lord, and all the families of the nations will bow down*

*before him, for dominion belongs to the Lord and he rules
over the nations."*                          Psalm 22:27-28
See also Psalm 67, 96, and 108

"Glory" is not only a *noun* describing God's revealed
qualities; it is also a *verb* meaning "to give praise, to
recognize and appreciate the worthiness of God." Out
of the overflow of his own reverence for the God he
loved, David set about to "glorify" God, to speak well of
his goodness to his children, to boast about his power, to
exult in his justice and his law, and to "glorify in his holy
name." (Psalm 105:3)

The ultimate expression of the glory of God was the
coming of Christ Jesus, the promised Messiah. John says
of Jesus:

> *"The Word became flesh and made his dwelling among us.
> We have seen his glory, the glory of the One and Only, who
> came from the Father, full of grace and truth."*
>
> John 1:14

The disciples determined to follow Jesus only after they
caught a glimpse of his glory, the reflection of his divine
power and character.

"Glorifying" is also an important concept in the life of
the early church. Those fledgling believers recognized
that the reputation of Jesus as the Son of God depended
on how well his character shone through in their lives.
His glory was enhanced when they brought others into

his kingdom, when they performed acts of mercy and kindness, and when their lives reflected the work of his Holy Spirit. They were keenly aware that their own character was being transformed "from one degree of glory to another."

On the negative side, David couldn't stand anything which would sully God's reputation or diminish his glory. His first appearance on the national scene was in the midst of a conflict between his own people and the neighboring Philistines. The Philistines seemed to have the military advantage, because one of their soldiers was a nine-foot giant named Goliath who challenged any Israelite to individual combat. They all prudently declined, based on their accurate assessment of Goliath's strength, size, and armament. But David viewed this giant from a totally different perspective: Goliath's offense was not that he threatened the security of Israel, but that he spoke poorly of God. He saw Goliath's taunts as an affront to God. His prior experience with God gave him the fierce confidence to confront this blasphemer. He looked Goliath in the eye and told him why he was about to die: "that all the earth may know that there is a God in Israel." (I Samuel 17:46b)

Third: David surrounded himself with strong friends by recruiting them to a cause which was greater than all of them put together. The cause was the success of the new kingdom of Israel, which David was convinced to be the chosen people of God. He poured his passion into that mission and called others to join him. Four hundred undesirables—debtors, malcontents, good-for-nothings—joined him in the Cave of Adullam when he was running for his life from King Saul, long before he himself was crowned king. David forged them into a formidable fighting force by holding high the banner of Israel's national destiny. He plunged confidently into battle against the enemies of Israel because he was on a mission from God. His total commitment motivated other men to join him in such a great effort.

As mentioned in the introduction, the term "undivided heart" occurs fourteen times in the Books of Kings and Chronicles. In all but one instance, an "undivided heart" refers to a person's allegiance to God. The one exception is found in I Chronicles 12:38 in which thousands of mighty warriors came to Hebron to swear their loyalty with "an undivided" heart to David. His undivided loyalty to God and God's people inspired their loyalty to him.

David also sought out strong spiritual leaders, men who were not afraid to confront him, like Samuel and Gad and Nathan. Unlike King Saul, who consulted advisors who told him only what he wanted hear, David wanted people around him who would speak the Word of God.

The contrast between David and Saul is stark: Saul had a *position* to protect, David had a *cause* to promote. Saul feared people who might jeopardize his authority; David welcomed people who balanced his strengths. Among his leaders, Saul had no giant-killers, because he had killed no giants himself. David had several generals who had slain giants. They willingly pledged their loyalty to a man who did not back down from giants.

A fourth lesson: David searched out the *ways* of God. He experienced the presence of God, he respected and kept the commands of God, and he witnessed the power of God, but he prayed earnestly to know the *ways* of God. God's ways are the means, the manner, the methods by which he accomplishes his desired objectives. David was eager to know not only *what* God was doing, but *how* he did it.

In the psalms, his lyrical prayers to God, David asked again and again,

> *"Show me your **ways**, O Lord, teach me your paths;"*
> Psalm 25:4

> *"Teach me your **way**, O Lord, and I will walk in your truth; give me an undivided heart, that I may fear your name."*          Psalm 86:11

David lived in constant awareness of the history of his people: how God had led them out of slavery in Egypt and how he wanted to give them an inheritance in the promised land of Canaan. In one of his psalms, David said,

> *"He made known his **ways** to Moses, his deeds to the people of Israel;..."*          Psalm 103:7

David appreciated the fact that Moses, the leader of that great exodus, sought out the *ways* of God. All the people of Israel were aware of *what* God was doing ("his deeds"), but Moses grasped *how* God was making it happen ("his ways").

However, because the people eventually scorned his *ways*, they were forced to wander in the wilderness for forty years. Moses should have known better, because he had been in such close fellowship with God that he should have conformed to God's means and methods.

Psalm 95 is a lament about Israel's foolishness concerning the ways of God. Because they did not do things God's way, one whole generation forfeited their opportunity to dwell in the Promised Land. The writer of the book of Hebrews in the New Testament elaborates on this psalm as an allegory of the spiritual life: God's people miss the blessing of the "Sabbath rest," the spirit-filled life, if they fail to seek and follow the *ways* of God. (Hebrews 3:1-4:12)

> *"That is why I was angry with that generation, and I said, 'Their hearts are always going astray, and they have not known my ways.' So I declared on oath in my anger, 'They shall never enter my rest.'"*          Hebrews 3:10-11

At the end of his life, when David was turning over the reins of leadership to his son Solomon, he charged Solomon:

*"So be strong, show yourself a man, and observe what the Lord your God requires: Walk in his **ways**, and keep his decrees and commands, his laws and requirements, as written in the Law of Moses, so that you may prosper in all you do and wherever you go, and that the Lord may keep his promise to me: 'If your descendants watch how they live, and if they walk faithfully before me with all their heart and soul, you will never fail to have a man on the throne of Israel.'"*        I Kings 2:3-4

Even in the construction of the temple, David knew that there were man's ways and God's ways. Man's way may be expedient, but God's way is eternal. Man's way may get the job done, but God's way gets the job done correctly. Man's way leaves destruction in its wake; God's way leaves "no sound of the hammer."

During his lifetime, David made a few errors in following the ways of God. One of the missions most important to him was bringing the ark of the covenant to Jerusalem. The Philistines had captured the ark and taken it home with them, but it caused them so much trouble they sent it back to southern Israel on a cart pulled by two milk cows yoked together. (I Samuel 6:7-8) David set the ark on a new cart, pulled by oxen and driven by Uzzah and Ahio, and led the procession toward Jerusalem. However, the oxen stumbled and Uzzah reached out to steady it. He was struck dead, and the whole parade was halted for months. David was furious! Wasn't this what God wanted—for the ark to be housed in Jerusalem? Yes, it was. Wasn't David's heart undivided in his loyalty to God?

Yes, it was. So, why was the project marred by tragedy? Because David failed to do it God's *way*.

God had given Moses explicit instructions about how the ark should be transported—by poles inserted through two rings built into each side of the ark and carried by priests (Exodus 25:14-15)—so this very kind of accident would not happen. David's goal was right and his motive was right. But he borrowed his methods, his *ways*, from the Philistines.

Much of the modern church suffers from the same lack of understanding of God's ways. They are good people, whose hearts are right toward God, doing what they believe to be God's will, but they borrow their methods from the Philistines, from the secular world. The Bible is their *message* book, but not their *method* book. Consequently, the church finds itself in the same state as the ark's procession: people are hurt, the leaders (like David) are angry and frustrated, and the mission is stalled.

David's yearning to know the *ways* of God found its fulfillment in the coming of Jesus, the son of David, the revelation of God in his fullness, who proclaimed, "I am the way." Not, "I will show you the way," or "I will teach you the way," but "I *am* the way." The Christians of the first century (as recorded in the Book of Acts) were called "followers of the Way." (Acts 9:2, 22:4, 24:14) And the gospel itself was referred to as "the Way." (Acts 19:9, 19:23, 24:22)

Despite his failures and faults, David set the standard for what it means to be "a man after God's own heart." He had an undivided loyalty to God, a passion for God's glory, and a focus on knowing the ways of his heavenly father. He was the model against which all the other kings of Judah would be measured. And, he is still a great example for those who follow in the steps of Jesus, the son of David, who commanded, "Seek first the kingdom of God and his righteousness..." (Matthew 6:33 KJV)

# CHAPTER 2

# Solomon: The Tragedy of a Divided Heart

*"I will give them an undivided heart and put a new spirit in them; I will remove from them their heart of stone and give them a heart of flesh. Then they will follow my decrees and be careful to keep my laws. They will be my people, and I will be their God. But as for those whose hearts are devoted to their vile images and detestable idols, I will bring down on their own heads what they have done, declares the Sovereign Lord."*
Ezekiel 11:19-21

The alignment of a person's heart will determine his or her destiny. We understand that. It makes sense. We know that the focus of our affections shapes our relationships with everyone else in our lives: spouse, children, friends, employees/employers, students/teachers, colleagues, and God. That's not hard to comprehend.

What is harder to grasp is that the quality of our heart bond to God affects many *other* people and may determine *their* destinies. How one person relates to God has a powerful impact on other family members, for example: not only our present family, but generations to come. An employer's heart-set influences a whole company. A teacher's walk with God, or lack of it, influences class after class of students. In some cases, one person's role in society is so significant that entire nations are affected— for good or evil. One of the most tragic examples of that truth is the story of Solomon.

Solomon had everything a person could ever want handed to him on a golden platter—not a silver platter, because he felt silver was an inferior metal to gold. So, he had everything in his house made of gold. He was the chosen successor to the kingdom of his father David, and he inherited the wealth and power and prestige of his father's legacy. Solomon grew up in David's palace, so his early life was one of privilege, culture, refinement, and religious observance. King David had set the example of an undivided heart to God before his son, and his constant prayer was that Solomon would have the same single-minded devotion that he had enjoyed throughout his lifetime.

Not only did Solomon inherit his father's kingdom, but his father's life mission as well: to build a temple for the worship of God. Even though the original vision was David's, God did not allow David to complete the mission because "there was too much blood on his hands." So, he handed the mission over to his son Solomon with specific instructions about how the temple should be constructed. Solomon accepted this assignment and fulfilled it faithfully, constructing a magnificent temple in which the Ark of the Covenant would rest and where the priestly functions of the nation could be performed.

According to Solomon's own account, God made two personal appearances to him during his lifetime. The first was a vision in which he dreamed that God gave him the opportunity to make one big wish. In his dream, Solomon asked for discernment in administering the affairs of the nation of Israel. He heard God say,

> *"Since you have asked for this and not for long life or wealth for yourself, nor have asked for the death of your enemies but for discernment in administering justice, I will do what you have asked. I will give you a wise and discerning heart, so that there will never have been anyone like you, nor will there ever be. Moreover, I will give you what you have not asked for—both riches and honor—so that in your lifetime you will have no equal among kings."*
>
> I Kings 3:11-13

It has always been assumed that Solomon made the right choice. Wrong! As the subsequent history of Israel proved, choosing wisdom was a good choice, but not the best. He should have asked for an undivided heart. Then, all the other benefits would have been his as well. But he didn't. He chose a lesser quality and paid dearly. His choice affected not only the people under his care at the time, but generations of the people of Israel. Seeking justice and knowledge and wisdom is a good thing, but without an undivided heart those pursuits have no lasting value.

King David had brought peace and prosperity to the nation by trusting God to give him military victory over Israel's pagan neighbors. Solomon also maintained peace and prosperity during the forty years of his rule, but through clever diplomacy rather than sheer trust in God. One of his first moves as king was to make an alliance with the Egyptian Pharaoh and to marry his daughter. (I Kings 3:1) This political marriage guaranteed peace on his southern border. He went on to marry many other wives from the royal families of surrounding nations. This may have seemed like a smart political move, but it was a tragic mistake. Those wives brought their religions with them and caused Solomon to lose his greatest possession: an undivided heart.

> *"King Solomon, however, loved many foreign women besides Pharaoh's daughter—Moabites, Ammonites, Edomites, Sidonians, and Hittites. They were from nations about which the Lord had told the Israelites, 'You must not intermarry with them, because they will surely turn your hearts after their gods.' Nevertheless, Solomon held fast to them in love. He had seven hundred wives of royal birth and three hundred concubines, and his wives led him astray. As Solomon grew old, his wives turned his heart after other gods, and his heart was not fully devoted to the Lord his God, as the heart of David his father had been.*

*He followed Ashtoreth the goddess of the Sidonians, and Molech the detestable god of the Ammonites. So Solomon did evil in the eyes of the Lord; he did not follow the Lord completely, as David his father had done."*

I Kings 11:1-6

As promised, God was angry with Solomon and declared that the kingdom would be torn away from him and given to one of his servants, not one of his sons. However, to keep his promise to David that one of his sons would sit on the throne forever, God retained one tribe to be ruled over by one of Solomon's sons. That one tribe would become the nation of Judah and would be known as "the southern kingdom."

From our vantage point nearly thirty centuries later, we may ask, "How did a person who had such opportunities, who knew exactly what God wanted and didn't want, who knew what would happen if a person turned to idols instead of the living God, who had such godly upbringing, who had a father who prayed specifically for an undivided heart, wind up doing the very thing he knew would be catastrophic?" We could ask the same question today of people who have access to the Word of God and who have the advantage of looking at Solomon as a bad example. What causes a person with such knowledge to forfeit the blessings of an undivided heart?

By studying Solomon's life story, we can identify some of the threats to an undivided heart:

1. He married wrong. In Solomon's case, he married
wrong many times. There were two things wrong with
his choice of wives: First, he married the wrong women
for the wrong reasons. His marriages were motivated, in
many cases, by political reasoning. Secondly, they were
not followers of the one true God. Marrying pagans was
absolutely prohibited by God. Solomon knew that. He
deliberately made a God-forbidden choice. Proof of
that is that he built the palace for his Egyptian queen far
away from the temple, because he knew it was a sacrilege
to bring pagan women into close proximity to the holy
temple of God. But he did it anyway, because his heart
was divided.

Unfortunately, Solomon's error is painfully common. So
often young people with a genuine zeal for the things of
God lose their spiritual vitality by marrying unbelievers.
Perhaps they think, "After we're married, she/he will
come to Christ by my example." Or even more foolishly,
"I'll help him get over his problems by marrying him."
In II Corinthians 6:14, we're warned not to be "yoked
together with unbelievers. For what do righteousness and
wickedness have in common? Or what fellowship can
light have with darkness?" The Apostle Paul goes on to
add that if a person turns to God, but his or her spouse
doesn't, that believer should live such an exemplary life
that the unbelieving spouse will be converted. However,
if a person who loves God has a choice, it should clearly
be one which honors God.

Some months ago, a pastor called me and asked to
discuss a personal issue. "I'm going through a slump in

my ministry and can't seem to get out of it. There's a lot of discontent in our church and complaints about my leadership. Could you give me some suggestions about how to get my ministry back on track?"

We met at a coffee shop, and I listened as he described the low level of spiritual vitality in his congregation. "What can I do to bring renewal to this church?"

Some church problems have logistical or demographic roots, but more often they are issues of the heart. So, I requested his permission to ask some "heart" questions: "Tell me how you came to faith in Christ, and how you felt called to Christian ministry."

Sure enough, according to his responses, he had had some deep personal encounters with Christ and had clearly sensed God's call to spiritual leadership.

So, I probed further. "Are you harboring any resentments or grudges or bitterness toward people who may have offended you?" (I always ask that question, because a "wounded heart" can be the root of lots of surface problems.) He thought for a moment, then said, "No, I can't think of any."

"Good," I said. "Are you involved in any relationships or habits that might damage your walk with the Lord?"

"Am I having an affair with someone? Is that what you're asking? The answer is 'Definitely, not.'"

"And how about habits?"

"Well," he admitted, "I do have a few little indulgences which some people in my church would frown at, but nobody knows about them, and they don't hurt anybody—and they don't cost anything."

I've heard this story before, so I had a suspicion about his "harmless indulgences." "Are you looking at sexual content on the internet?"

"Like I said," he explained, "nobody knows about it. Not even my wife. And it doesn't cost anything."

My next question took him aback: "These women, the ones you are visualizing having sex with, are they all Christians?"

"That's a ridiculous question! I don't even know who they are. It's not about them. I'm just fulfilling my own needs."

"That's what Solomon said. You remember Solomon— the man who claimed to be the smartest man in the world. He brought those women into his life, and it cost him his most valuable possession. I'm afraid it's costing you dearly."

He was defensive. "If you're suggesting that this is ruining my marriage, you're wrong. My wife and I have never been happier with each other. Our marriage is fine."

"I'm not talking about your marriage," I said. "Your most valuable possession is an undivided heart, and your heart has been divided by women you don't even know."

He was huffy. "I've been at this church eleven years. We've had ups and downs, and I'll admit that we're in a low place now, but I've weathered these storms before, and I'll get through this one."

One month later, I learned that he had been dismissed from his pastorate and had moved to another city. It may be that he has found a successful ministry somewhere else, but I do know that the Lord will not bless the work of a man with a divided heart.

2. There is a vast difference between reverence for God and communion with God. Solomon was faithful to carry out his mission for God: to build the temple. He urged his people to obey the commandments of God and to remember their spiritual heritage. His prayers at the dedication of the temple are very nice prayers, theologically correct, and accurate in their testimony to God's faithfulness to Israel. But they lack the spiritual passion of David. In none of the historical accounts of Solomon's life do we read of the kind of intimate fellowship with God his father enjoyed.

There is always a temptation among people who have grown up in godly homes to substitute the outward trappings of religion for personal bonding with God.

3. It is difficult for a person who inherits wealth to sense a need for God. David learned to trust in God's provision when he had nothing, when he was not even sure his life would be spared. That sense of dependency continued throughout his life. Solomon never knew want; he never was thrown on the mercy of God for survival.

Jesus said it is harder for a rich man to enter the kingdom than for a camel to go through the eye of a needle. Paul wrote to Timothy about the dangers of seeking wealth:

> *"People who want to get rich fall into temptation and a trap and into many foolish and harmful desires that plunge men into ruin and destruction. For the love of money is a root of all kinds of evil. Some people, eager for money, have wandered from the faith and pierced themselves with many griefs."*                    I Timothy 6:9-10

Solomon had a perfect opportunity to convert an unbeliever to faith in God when the Queen of Sheba came for a visit. She specifically asked about the relationship between a personal friendship with God and material wealth. Solomon impressed her with his learning and wisdom and especially with his ostentatious display of wealth. However, in the end she went away with an appreciation only for the blessings of God, not with a desire to know God personally.

4. Solomon did not serve an apprenticeship in difficult surroundings like David did. David was not born a king; he worked his way up from the bottom of society's

ladder—tending sheep. It was there his character was molded and his faith established. He had to fight his way into leadership, leading his men through conquest and defeat. We have no record of Solomon going to war with his armies. He directed them from the palace.

Jesus outlined the curriculum for spiritual leaders:

> *"Whoever can be trusted with very little can also be trusted with much, and whoever is dishonest with very little will also be dishonest with much. So if you have not been trustworthy in handling worldly wealth, who will trust you with true riches? And if you have not been trustworthy with someone else's property, who will give you property of your own?"*
>
> Luke 16:10-12

Many people aspire to spiritual leadership but are unwilling to go through the rigors of starting with small things, material things, and things that are someone else's before moving up to their own ministry.

Every person has a circle of influence. Regardless of wealth, position, training, or intellectual capacity, everyone affects someone else—or many others. The breadth of that circle may be determined by many factors, but the quality of our spiritual impact is decided by one factor: the degree to which a person does or does not have an undivided heart.

If, in our lifetime, one person comes to wholehearted faith in God, that contribution is of greater long-term value than winning a million votes in the next election or selling more vacuum cleaners than anyone else in Wisconsin. Each of us is responsible for the depth of our influence on other people. God alone is responsible for the breadth of our service.

# Chapter 3

# Asa: Finishing Well

*"You need to persevere so that when you have done the will of God, you will receive what he has promised."*

Hebrews 10:36

Asa was one of the first kings of Judah (actually the third), but we should consider his story last because of the life message he left us. He ruled in Jerusalem as king for 41 years and was a great king for 36 of those years. Then, at the end of his life, he messed up. Instead of relying on God—the God who had given him so many years of success and victory—he tried to make things happen in his own strength. The consequences were tragic. This great king, who could have gone out in a blaze of glory, went down in the smoke of shame and regret. He finished poorly.

Let's look at the great years first: from the outset he "did what was right in the eyes of the Lord." He removed all the symbols of idolatry from Judah and repaired the temple of the Lord. One of the most courageous acts was to remove his own grandmother, Maacah, from her position as queen mother because she put up an Asherah pole—a symbol of a pagan god. (I Kings 15:13, II Chronicles 15:16) He cut the detestable thing down, chopped it into pieces, and burned it in the Kidron Valley. Way to go, Asa!

A key role in Asa's early success was his responsiveness to the messenger of the Lord, who happened to be a prophet named Azariah. Azariah delivered a "word from the Lord" which is a wonderful summary of God's relationship to his people during the whole history of Judah:

> *"Listen to me, Asa and all Judah and Benjamin. The Lord is with you when you are with him. If you seek him, he will be found by you, but if you forsake him, he will forsake you. For a long time Israel was without the true God, without a priest to teach and without the law. But in their distress they turned to the Lord, the God of Israel, and sought him, and he was found by them. In those days it was not safe to travel about, for all the inhabitants of the lands were in great turmoil. One nation was being crushed by another and one city by another, because God was troubling them with every kind of distress. But as for you, be strong and do not give up, for your work will be rewarded."*
>
> II Chronicles 15:2-7

All the great themes of the Books of Chronicles are wrapped up in this succinct pronouncement:

1. If you seek God, you will find him and be blessed.
2. If you forsake God, he will forsake you, and the consequences will be very unpleasant.
3. If you know God's law, it will lead to safety and success.
4. There are plenty of historical examples of people who forsook God and found themselves in "turmoil" and "distress."
5. Even if you mess up, God will straighten things out if you turn to him.
6. For these reasons, you should take courage and press on. God will reward your efforts.

This is a good place to review the role played by spiritual leaders in enabling God's people to have undivided hearts. None of us is strong enough to fight the battle alone. We do not have the ability to pull ourselves up by our own bootstraps. We are not self-made men (or women). On our own, even though we trust in God, we lack the power to withstand severe trials, temptations, and difficulties. That is why God has provided spiritual advisors to remind us of his strength and our weakness. We need to pay attention to the messengers of God. We need to hear this message on a regular basis: "Seek God with an undivided heart and you will find him. He will be the source of your strength. If you are already reaping the consequences of your own wrong behavior, repent and turn to God. And take courage! Don't give up!"

That is exactly what Asa did. He "took courage" to carry out the work God had given him, not only to lead his people but to cleanse the land of evil practices and false worship. Armed with the assurance that God's work would prevail, he went about his work with confidence, and the results were very satisfying.

But then, in his old age, Asa did a very foolish thing. The king of the northern kingdom, Israel, began to fortify the city of Ramah on Judah's northern boundary. If he had succeeded, this would have effectively blockaded Judah from trade with the outside world and given the enemy a foothold to attack Judah. So, what should King Asa do? From our enlightened historical perspective, and based on all he had been taught, Asa should have trusted God to remedy the dilemma. However, he trusted his own ingenuity instead.

Asa took all the silver and gold which had been stored in the temple and in his own palace and cut a deal with the king of Aram (now Syria). "See, I am sending you silver and gold. Now, break your treaty with Baasha, King of Israel, so he will withdraw from me." It seemed to work. The Israelites abandoned their fortification of Ramah, and the men of Judah carried off all the stones and timbers they had assembled there and fortified their own cities. Clever, right? No, it was foolish. Asa should have trusted God for his safety, not the Arameans.

Again, and true to fashion, God sent a messenger to Asa to express his anger. Hanani, the seer, confronted him:

*"Because you relied on the king of Aram and not on the Lord your God, the army of the king of Aram has escaped from your hand. Were not the Cushites and Libyans a mighty army with great numbers of chariots and horsemen? Yet when you relied on the Lord, he delivered them into your hand. For the eyes of the Lord range throughout the earth to strengthen those whose hearts are fully committed to him. You have done a foolish thing, and from now on you will be at war."* II Chronicles 16:7-9

Asa was like a racehorse who leads the field through most of the race. The crowd is on its feet, cheering him on to victory. But at the last turn, something happens. In the final stretch, he folds. Just when victory was his, he wound up losing.

The last years of Asa's reign are a disaster. Instead of listening to Hanani, he had him thrown into prison. He vented his anger by brutally oppressing some of his own people. And when he developed a serious disease in his feet, he failed to turn to God for healing. He could have gone out in glory; instead he went down in defeat.

Contrast this with the testimony of one of God's leaders in the New Testament, the Apostle Paul, who faced just as serious calamities in his later years:

*"For I am already being poured out like a drink offering, and the time has come for my departure. I have fought the good fight, I have finished the race, I have kept the faith. Now there is in store for me the crown of righteousness,*

*which the Lord, the righteous Judge, will award to me on that day—and not only to me, but also to all who have longed for his appearing."*                    II Timothy 4:6-8

Throughout this study, we have used the words of Hanani as a promise from God:

*"For the eyes of the Lord range throughout the earth to strengthen those whose hearts are fully committed (undivided) to him."*                    II Chronicles 16:9

It *is* a promise, but in Asa's case it was also an indictment. The Word of God is a two-edged sword: a promise to those who apply it and a warning to those who don't.

I was fortunate to have many Christian friends in high school, college, and graduate school. In the years since graduation, I have been pleased to hear reports that many of my classmates have gone on to spiritual maturity, a fulfilling walk with Christ, and productive Christian service. However, there were some of my friends who started well but finished poorly. Like King Asa, at some critical juncture in their lives they chose to trust in their own cleverness rather than the God who had guided them and empowered them in their early years.

Just recently, I learned that one of my college buddies had died. We had trained together for Christian service, and in our college years he had been considered "the most likely to succeed." I called a mutual friend who had known him in his later years, and I asked, "Did he die well?" "No," he said, "he certainly did not." I grieved for my friend, but I prayed for myself: "Oh, God, I know how easy it would be at this stage of my life to become complacent in my walk with you. Remind me of my weakness, and keep me dependent on your guidance and strength. O, may I finish well."

The great truths of God are timeless. They apply to every person in every era of human history. They are as applicable today as in the days of the kings of Judah. Those historical narratives are rich resources for us to encourage us in our pursuit of an undivided heart toward God. They are also historical proof that God's wrath will be poured out on those who defy his ways and turn their hearts to other gods.

The message we should glean from the study of these kings is that God is eagerly seeking a love relationship with people. He is offering the blessing of covenant friendship with him to those who will seek him—on his own terms. At this moment, today, the eyes of the Lord are still looking for those whose hearts are loyal to him. He delights in showing himself strong on their behalf.

The American evangelist Dwight L. Moody was a shoe salesman in Chicago who was converted and dedicated his life to God. He began his ministry with a Sunday School class for newsboys, then God expanded his ministry to bring thousands to faith in Christ. His motto was, "The world has yet to see what God can do through one person who is totally committed to him. By God's grace, I intend to be that person."

# CHAPTER 4

# Jehoshaphat: Great Heart, Bad Friends, Terrible Combination

*"Do not be yoked together with unbelievers. For what do righteousness and wickedness have in common? Or what fellowship can light have with darkness?"*

II Corinthians 6:14

Jehoshaphat was a fine man and a great king. He could have gone down in history in the same league as David or Hezekiah or Josiah. He certainly had an undivided heart toward God. He continued the spiritual reforms his father Asa had begun, and he added some new values to the quality of life in the kingdom of Judah. However, Jehoshaphat had a fatal flaw—one that plagues

well-meaning believers today. He got into alliances with
ungodly partners, and it cost him dearly. One of his
"deals" caused him great financial loss, one nearly got
him killed, but one devastated the whole nation of Judah.
It wiped out all the good that he had done. It destroyed
his whole legacy.

The chronicler says some wonderful things about
Jehoshaphat. What father wouldn't love to hear these
things reported about his son?

- "The Lord was with him"
- "He walked in the ways of his father David"
- "He sought the God of his fathers and
  followed his commands"
- "His heart was devoted to the ways of the
  Lord" (II Chronicles 17:3-6)

The overflow of Jehoshaphat's character was his success
as a king:

- The Lord established the kingdom under his
  control
- All the people brought gifts to him, so he had
  great wealth and honor
- The fear of the Lord fell on all his enemies,
  and they brought him gifts (II Chronicles
  17:5-11)

Jehoshaphat introduced some very creative services for
the people of Judah. First, he sent well-trained teachers
throughout the nation to instruct the people in the

Law of the Lord. (II Chronicles 17:7-9) This is the first mention in human history of what we know now as "extension education." Priests and Levites accompanied the teachers to explain the practical application of God's Word to everyday life. Secondly, he established a network of judges throughout the land to administer justice, settle disputes, and help the people comply with God's revealed standards. Both were great ideas. (II Chronicles 19:4-11)

The geo-political situation which Jehoshaphat inherited was precarious: Judah was a small, independent nation made up of the two tribes of Judah and Benjamin, plus quite a few Levites who had fled the northern kingdom of Israel. It had been founded by those faithful people of God who were loyal to the family of David and to the worship of the true God of Abraham, Isaac, and Jacob. Jerusalem was its capital. When Jehoshaphat became king, Judah already had a track record of sixty years as an independent nation, mostly good years of peace and prosperity—because they did things God's way.

Judah was a land-locked kingdom about forty miles square. They were bounded on the north by the nation of Israel, the ten tribes which had rejected the leadership of David's family. To the east were the Moabites, who were under the control of the empire of the Assyrians, and to the south and west were various tribes of people loyal to the dynasty of Egypt. They were all hostile to Judah, and their armies kept probing Judah's borders for weakness, looking for opportunity to conquer territory.

From the time they separated into two kingdoms, there was tension between Israel and Judah. The kings of Israel reinforced their borders with Judah and kept trying to push southward by taking one village after another.

The much larger nation of Israel was experiencing a boom of both prosperity and power by reason of their strategic alliance with the empire of the Assyrians. They were allied with another of Assyria's vassal states, Phoenicia—a nation known for its sea-faring trade with all the nations which had ports on the Mediterranean Sea.

Jehoshaphat was keenly aware of his delicate situation. Yes, God had protected and provided for Judah for sixty years, but the presence of such powerful and rich nations on his borders must have caused him great concern. In this crucible, Jehoshaphat made some terrible mistakes of judgment. It would help us if we could get into his mind and understand the pressures he was under, but who can understand what motivated a king 2,800 years ago? From our historical vantage point, we must wonder why he would give in to the temptation to form friendships with nations who were under the judgment of God. Why would he do this? If God had been faithful to his covenant to protect and provide, why should Jehoshaphat feel the need to "cover his bases" by making alliances with ungodly rulers and businessmen? Sad to say, he did both. He arranged a marriage between his first-born son Jehoram and the daughter of the Phoenician king for business opportunities, and he entered into a military alliance with Israel for protection.

Ahab, the king of Israel, had taken over from his father Omri. To enhance his opportunities for international trade, Ahab had married the daughter of the Phoenician king. Her name was Jezebel. The partnership seemed to be working. Jezebel was an ardent proponent of Baal worship, and she had imported 450 priests of Baal from Phoenicia to promote that religion in Israel. Ahab tolerated it because, businesswise, he had no choice. There was constant religious conflict internally in Israel, but outwardly the nation was prosperous. Jezebel also encouraged her husband Ahab in power-grabbing business deals, like stealing the vineyard of Naboth. (I Kings 21:1-29)

Here was Jehoshaphat's first big wrong decision: Impressed by how Ahab had prospered by marrying Jezebel, he arranged for his first-born son Jehoram to marry Athaliah, the daughter of Ahab and Jezebel. Big mistake! The tragic consequences did not show up right away, but the influence Athaliah would have on Jehoshaphat's son would have devastating consequences for the people of Judah. Athaliah shared her mother's devotion to Baal, and she promoted that disgusting religion through her role as Jehoram's wife.

So, now that they were officially related by the marriage of their children, Jehoshaphat paid a visit to King Ahab at his palace up in Israel. Ahab flattered him with praise and a lavish feast, then presented a proposal: "Now that our children are married to each other, let's join forces against one of my enemies, the Arameans at Raboth Gilead."

Jehoshaphat jumped at the opportunity. "Sure! Your people and my people were originally one, so let's do it!" Then, remembering his spiritual roots, he said, "Wait a minute! I'd better get some counsel from the Lord on this first. Do you have any prophets up here in Israel?"

"Of course we have prophets," Ahab replied. "Here are 400 of them. Let's see what they say."

Sure enough, all of Ahab's prophets agreed that God was favorable to the plan. "Go!" they said, "for God will give the battle into the king's hand."

Jehoshaphat felt that check in his spirit we all feel when we sense something is not right. "Don't you have any more prophets?" he asked.

"Yes," said Ahab, "there is one more, but he always brings me bad news, so I hate him. His name is Micaiah."

While the other prophets were doing a victory dance in anticipation of a victory at Ramoth Gilead, Micaiah prophesied the opposite. To make a long, but interesting, story short, Ahab had Micaiah thrown into prison, and he and Jehoshaphat went on to war with the Arameans.

Ahab thought he had a clever plan to save his own hide. He knew that the Aramean king hated him and would order his troops to target him personally. So he told Jehoshaphat, "You go into battle in your royal robes, and I'll wear a disguise so they won't recognize me." What was Jehoshaphat thinking to agree to a plan like that? Anyway, as soon as the battle commenced, the Aramean charioteers chased the one who looked like a king. Just when they were about to kill him, Jehoshaphat cried out and they gave up the chase. Close call! Unfortunately for Ahab, his disguise didn't protect him. A random arrow pierced between the plates of his armor and he was mortally wounded. The words of Micaiah the prophet rang true: "Israel will be scattered like sheep without a shepherd."

When Jehoshaphat returned home to Judah, one of his own prophets, Jehu, confronted him: "How stupid can you be? The Lord is pleased that you seek him and destroy the pagan idols, but you have done something that really angers him! You have helped wicked people and linked up with people who hate God." (II Chronicles 19:1-3, my translation) Did Jehoshaphat learn his lesson? Yes, he learned to trust the Lord for protection against his enemies, but no, he still hankered after trade with the Phoenicians. Hoping to cash in on the lucrative Mediterranean trade, he and the ungodly king of Israel invested in a fleet of ships. The bottom line in that deal: they all were wrecked before they even set sail. It was a serious financial loss.

This is a hard chapter for me to write because I have seen so many of my friends make the same mistake. Good, godly men—men who have served God's kingdom well—become "unequally yoked" in business or marriage, just like Jehoshaphat. They may even have been encouraged by "spiritual advisors," just like the prophets who told Jehoshaphat to join Ahab in battle.

One time I was leading a Bible study for Christian businessmen. We were working through the II Corinthian passage about not being "unequally yoked." Thinking someone might have a personal experience to illustrate the danger, I asked, "Has anyone here paid dearly for getting into a deal with people who did not share your Christian values?" Every hand went up, including mine! The temptation is universal, but the consequences are predictable. Just don't do it.

The lure of business deals with unbelievers is costly enough, but the penalties for marrying someone who has rejected God are far more serious. Jehoshaphat had wisely set up a good succession plan. He knew that "success without a successor is failure." He had given each of his sons—Jehoram, Azariah, Jehiel, Zechariah, Azariahu, Michael, and Shephatiah—on-the-job training in civic leadership. He gave each of them a fortified city to govern and the resources they needed. Surely one of them—or several of them—would continue the good policies Jehoshaphat had put in place.

When it came time to appoint one of them to be the next king, he chose Jehoram because he was the first born. But remember: Jehoram was married to Athaliah, daughter of Jezebel—Baal worshipper, Phoenician, and a murderous schemer, just like her mother. As soon as Jehoram was firmly in control, he murdered all the other sons of Jehoshaphat. He led the whole nation into idolatry, establishing "high places" for Baal worship in all the towns of Judah. The peace Judah had enjoyed began to unravel. The Edomites rebelled and set up their own kingdom. The people of Libnah revolted.

Finally, Elijah the prophet sent a letter to Jehoram. It was his death sentence:

> *"This is what the Lord, the God of your father David, says: 'You have not walked in the ways of your father Jehoshaphat or of Asa king of Judah. But you have walked in the ways of the kings of Israel, and you have led Judah and the people of Jerusalem to prostitute themselves, just as the house of Ahab did. You have also murdered your own brothers, members of your father's house, men who were better than you. So now the Lord is about to strike your people, your sons, your wives and everything that is yours, with a heavy blow. You yourself will be very ill with a lingering disease of the bowels, until the disease causes your bowels to come out.'"*          II Chronicles 21:12-15

Invaders pushed in from every side. They ransacked Judah and carried off everything of value. Jehoram's own sons and their wives were all taken away—except Azariah, the youngest one (so God's promise to maintain David's line would be assured). Jehoram died a painful and tragic death, and he was buried in shame and dishonor. His epitaph is the saddest any person could receive:

> *"...he passed away, to no one's regret..."*
>
> II Chronicles 21:20

Marriage is the ultimate spiritual partnership. It is supposed to be a picture on earth of God's family in heaven. Through marriage, we pass on the legacy of God's blessing from one generation to the next. We dare not trifle with the destinies of those who will follow us by entering into or encouraging marriages with unbelievers. So many times I have heard parents lament, "We knew that the fellow our daughter wanted to marry was not a Christian, but we hoped that she could have a good influence on him. He came from such a_____(fill in the blank: wealthy, prominent, well-educated, respected) family." The heritage of faith that had been passed down from one generation to the next was forgotten by their grandchildren. What a loss!

If Jehoshaphat could come back to us today and tell us what lesson he had learned, I'm confident he would say, "Don't link up with people who have rejected God."

# CHAPTER 5

# Joash: Second-Hand Religion

Nobody came from a more dysfunctional family than Joash, seventh king of Judah. His father Ahaz was a bad king who ruled in Jerusalem only one year before he was killed. His own grandmother, Athaliah, was worse. You remember Athaliah: she was the daughter of Jezebel. As soon as her husband was dead, she seized the throne of Judah. She set about to murder every remaining member of the royal family of David, forty-one of them, including her own grandchildren. Only one escaped. His name was Joash, and he was just a baby at the time. He was rescued by a godly aunt, Jehoshiba, and her husband Jehoiada, a priest. They hid him in a bedroom while all his relatives were being slaughtered, then raised him secretly in the Temple. (II Chronicles 22:10-12)

For the next seven years, the wicked grandmother Athaliah ruled Judah while Jehoiada and Jehoshiba were secretly raising young Joash. They were grooming him to be a godly king. When he was seven years old, Jehoiada arranged for him to be anointed king over Judah. Of course Athaliah was furious, but she was outnumbered by the people who were loyal to the family of David and she was killed.

Now Judah was ready for a great renewal. Jehoiada and Joash led the people in making a covenant to serve God and to turn away from the worship of Baal. They smashed the altars and idols of this false god and killed the pagan priests. Young Joash was right in the middle of all this. Jehoiada led and Joash followed. Jehoiada even chose wives for him: godly ladies all, no doubt. It was Joash's own idea to restore the temple to its former glory, and it was he who came up with the idea of placing an offering box at the gate of the temple.

Scripture records that:

> *"Joash did right in the eyes of the Lord all the years of Jehoiada the priest."*   II Chronicles 24:2

There's the catch: "all the years of Jehoiada the priest." Unfortunately, as soon as Jehoiada died, Joash went in the opposite direction. Officials of his court "paid homage to him." (II Chronicles 24:17) I suppose that means they influenced him with their flattery. Whatever they said, the chronicler records that "he listened to them." He turned his back on the God of David and restored idol worship in Judah.

At this point, the story of Joash follows a familiar, but tragic, trajectory:

1. God became angry with him and sent a prophet to warn him.
2. The prophet was Zechariah, Jehoiada's only son. The Word of the Lord he brought was, "Why do you disobey the Lord's commands? You will not prosper. Because you have forsaken the Lord, he has forsaken you." (II Chronicles 24:20)
3. At this point Joash could have repented and been restored to God's favor. However, Joash not only failed to repent, he ordered the prophet killed, stoned to death in the courtyard of the Temple. Centuries later, Jesus would use this murder of Zechariah as an example of what evil people have done to God's messengers. (Matthew 23:35 and Luke 11:51)
4. As a consequence of his refusal to repent, God sent the army of the Arameans against Joash's much larger army, and (you guessed it), the army of Judah was soundly defeated. Joash was seriously wounded and taken back to Jerusalem. It seemed that he had at least escaped with his life, but his associates were so angry that Joash had murdered Jehoiada's son they killed him in his bed. He was not even allowed to have a tomb among the great kings

of Judah because he had turned away from God.

Joash is a tragic example of secondhand religion. As long as he was carried along by Jehoiada, he did what was right. But as soon as his spiritual mentor was gone, he turned against the God he had served. Unfortunately, many Christians today are "hothouse" believers, much like plants which thrive in the greenhouse but wither and die when they are transplanted into a harsher environment outdoors.

We have a friend who grew up in a great church. The pastor of that church took him into his own home, treating him like one of his own sons. In that environment, he was a model Christian: serving, witnessing to his faith, and taking an active role in the life of the church. However, every time he left that protective environment, he fell away into a worldly lifestyle. Every time he returned, he resumed his Christian persona. His problem was secondhand religion. Unfortunately, the greatest trial of his life, the death of his daughter, caught him at a time when he was out from under the protective the umbrella of the pastor's home. He fell apart and never recovered, because he had no spiritual roots of his own. How sad!

Could Jehoiada have done anything differently to prepare young Joash to stand alone? More importantly for us, is there anything we can do today to prepare believers who are nurtured in a protective environment for life in a hostile society? I believe there is a method, illustrated in the narratives of the New Testament, but it comes with a risk: some followers may fall away in the process. When the gardener transplants seedlings from the hothouse to the outdoor garden, some plants succumb to the elements.

Both Jesus and Paul modeled this method in the training of their colleagues. I call the process "guided missions." Here is what Jesus practiced with two sets of his followers, the original twelve disciples (Matthew 10:5-15, Luke 9), then seventy more (Luke 10:1-20). He sent them on carefully prescribed mission assignments. He gave them a clear task: "Go into the towns and villages of Judea and announce that the Kingdom of God has come." He gave them clear instructions: "Go two by two. Don't take any money, extra clothes, food, or weapons." He gave them a clear plan: "Find a 'man of peace' and stay at his house. Work out from there, doing good and announcing the kingdom." And, he gave them a clear warning: "Some places won't accept you. If they don't, leave that place and go somewhere else."

When each group returned, Jesus took them to a secluded place for a de-briefing (Luke 10:17): "What happened? What did you learn?" In each case they reported that they had discovered the power of ministering in Jesus' name.

Paul followed the same course with young Timothy. First he took him on a mission trip, modeling what it meant to proclaim the gospel in an unfriendly setting. Then he sent him on a series of guided missions: first simply to deliver letters to the struggling churches and bring back a report, then to bring back funds, and finally to sort out problems in those churches. Apparently the turmoil at the church in Corinth was too overwhelming for timid Timothy, so Paul had to send the next letter (II Corinthians) with Titus. Eventually, Paul was able to send Timothy to the Philippian church with this recommendation: "I have no one else like him, who takes a genuine interest in your welfare." (Philippians 2:20) Timothy eventually became the pastor or bishop of the great church at Ephesus. Paul had taken a shy teenager from a broken home to spiritual leadership through a series of carefully planned exercises.

It must be admitted that there were several casualties in both Jesus' and Paul's "guided missions." Paul mentions by name some of those who crashed spiritually, like Phygellus and Hernogenes (II Timothy 1:15), Demas, (II Timothy 4:10), "having loved this present world," and Hymenaus and Alexander (I Timothy 1:18-20), "who made a shipwreck of their faith."

Not every mentor has the same intensity as the Apostle Paul. His standard was "sink or swim!" That was not the style of his colleague Barnabas, and they had a serious disagreement about how to handle someone who couldn't stand the pressure. Paul refused to take young John Mark with him on a mission to Syria and Cilicia because he had bailed out on an earlier mission (Acts 13:13). "I won't have a quitter on my team!" he said. Barnabas thought differently, and he took John Mark under his wing. Fortunately, Mark thrived under Barnabas' tutelage, so much so that Paul said later, "Bring Mark with you. He is a valuable man to the ministry." (II Timothy 4:11)

A wise disciple-builder gives assignments to those he is mentoring, which will lead to independent confidence in God's provision and care. With proper guidelines and follow-up, those assignments will help them build a personal interactive friendship with God. Then when the mentor—like Jehoiada, Paul, or even Jesus in the flesh— is absent, they have deep resources of spiritual strength to carry them through.

# CHAPTER 6

# Amaziah: The Double-Minded King

*"I hate double-minded men, but I love your law."*
Psalm 119:113

Amaziah was a tragic figure. He was outwardly religious, but his heart wasn't in it. His faith was formal, but not personal. He "talked the talk, but he didn't walk the walk." The chronicler tells us:

> *"He did what was right in the eyes of the Lord, but not wholeheartedly."*　II Chronicles 25:2

The Hebrew phrase used here to describe what Amaziah didn't have is *lev shalame*—an undivided heart. What he did have was a puffed up opinion of himself and his abilities. He had grandiose plans and excessive ambition. He wanted to go down in history as a conquering hero, as King David had done, but he lacked the one quality that would bring him success: total loyalty to God

Despite his hubris, the writer of Chronicles affirms that, at least outwardly, "he did what was right in the sight of the Lord." If he lacked devotion for God, why would he even try to do what was right? Perhaps the answer lies in his upbringing. Remember that Amaziah was the son of Joash, the king who started so well and ended so poorly. Imagine what it must have been like to grow up in a home with a dad who had murdered the prophet of God and turned his back on God's ways. Amaziah must have been sobered by the calamity caused by his father's abandoning his own childhood faith and rebelling against God. So, perhaps remembering his father's fate, Amaziah made a public declaration of his allegiance to God and God's ways. However, he was like a lot of "good 'ol boys" in politics today who pay lip-service to God and traditional (religious) values, but whose hearts are bent on selfish ambitions and worldly pursuits.

Everything Amaziah attempted turned out badly. First, he drafted an army—every able-bodied man over twenty years of age in Judah—far more than he needed to protect the nations' borders. Once they were ready to fight, he looked around for an easy adversary. He decided to attack the Edomites, who lived south of Judah near the Dead Sea. These were the descendents of Esau (Genesis 25:30) who had refused the Israelites passage through their land on their way from Egypt to the Promised Land. (Numbers 20:18-20) Thinking his own army might not be sufficient, Amaziah made a deal to hire 100,000 mercenaries from the northern kingdom, Israel.

Bad choice! Israel was at that time under the judgment of God—not the kind of ally anyone would want. Amaziah should have known this, but God had to send a prophet to explain why any such an arrangement was doomed to failure. So, grudgingly, Amaziah sent the mercenaries home, complaining to the prophet: "But what about the money? I paid 100 talents (3.4 metric tons) of silver for them!"

Nevertheless, Amaziah went off to fight the Edomites in the Valley of Salt without the help of the hired mercenaries. The campaign seemed to be successful except for two things:

1. The 100,000 disgruntled mercenaries from Israel *did* go home, but on the way they plundered several cities of Judah. They killed 3,000 innocent citizens and carried off all their possessions.
2. Amaziah was so proud he had defeated the Edomites that he brought their gods home with him. Since he won them as trophies in battle, he decided to make them his own gods, to bow down to them, and to make sacrifices to them. (II Chronicles 25:14) Another bad idea!

As is the pattern all through Chronicles, God was angry with him and sent a prophet to give him an opportunity to repent. The prophet said,

> *"How stupid can you be? Why are you bowing down to an idol of the Edomites who couldn't even save them from yourself?"*     II Chronicles 25:15, my translation

If Amaziah's heart had been open to God's voice, he would have been responsive to what the prophet spoke. Instead, he retorted,

> *"Who made you an advisor to the king? Do you want me to smack you down?"*
>     II Chronicles 25:16, my translation

The prophet didn't say any more, except,

> *"Let's see who gets smacked down. I told you the truth, and you wouldn't listen."*
>     II Chronicles 25:16, again, my translation

Poor Amaziah! He was the prisoner of his own foolishness. His "victory" against the Edomites convinced him he was an invincible warrior, surely capable of conquering other nations. Full of bravado, he picked a fight with Israel, Judah's neighbor to the north: "Come out and fight me, face to face!" he said.

Jehoash, king of Israel, replied:

*"You're all puffed up with pride because you defeated the Edomites. Your arrogance is getting the best of you. Just stay at home and don't cause trouble. It will only bring you grief."*     II Chronicles 25:19, my translation

Do you think Amaziah listened? No, he engaged the army of Israel at Beth Shemesh and was soundly defeated. The chronicler says,

*"Every man fled to his own home."*
II Chronicles 25:22

Every man, that is, except Amaziah. Jehoash caught him and dragged him back into Jerusalem. He made him watch while his men plundered the city.

*"Do you like this wall around your city? Watch this!" And Jehoash's men tore down 600 feet of the wall from the Ephraim Gate to the Corner Gate. "Nice silver and gold you have here," he said, and he gathered it all up and took it to his own house in Samaria. "I think I'll take all the articles out of the Temple and some hostages, too, just in case you want to try this again."*
II Chronicles 25:23-24, my translation

Amaziah ruled for 29 years, but it was not a happy time. His own citizens had no respect for him and conspired against him. In desperation, he fled to the town of Lachish, thinking that would be a safe haven. However, his enemies at home in Jerusalem sent assassins and killed him there. Amaziah's body was brought back on horseback and was buried.

Amaziah was a pitiful character: his outward profession did not match the reality of his inner life. He was torn between his own ambitions and what he knew to be the "ways of God." He was what is called in the New Testament as a "double minded man." It is a miserable way to live.

Sad to say, there are still several kinds of "Amaziahs":

1. People who use religious pretension to gain power or prestige. Jesus had frequent confrontations with a religious party known as the Pharisees. Some of these folks were fastidious about keeping the Jewish ceremonial law and "did what was right," but their hearts were not tender toward God. (Matthew 23:13-39) Their public displays of piety were calculated to give them a sense of superiority over ordinary people. Jesus knew the self-centeredness in their hearts, and he correctly identified them as hypocrites.

2. A second group of "Amaziahs" is what I would call "cultural Christians." They have grown up in a Christian culture and live by accepted norms. They are church-attenders, moral, upright, and respectable citizens, but they have no heart-felt devotion to God. They are often wonderful people, but they are missing so much! There is no joy in their worship, no delight in the service they offer, and no eagerness about the anticipation of eternal life. They are good church members. There is nothing

"wrong" with them. They're just not spiritually alive. They are not deliberate deceivers, not willful hypocrites. They simply lack spiritual vitality.

3. Some double-minded people are that way because they just can't decide. They are sincerely drawn to the things of God, but they are also attracted to the values and ways of the world. They are torn between the two kingdoms and cannot bring themselves to make the choice. If they throw themselves with abandon on the grace of God, they will forfeit the pleasures of the world. If they jettison their Christian appearances, they will face the disapproval of their friends, family, and community. They have a foot in both worlds, but no success or satisfaction in either. They are what is called "lukewarm."

The Apostle James warned the early Christians about the dangers of double-mindedness. In the opening paragraph of his letter to the church, he described the plight of the double-minded person: he is unstable in all his ways, tossed every which way like waves blown by the wind. He has no right to expect anything from God, because God will not waste his resources on fence-straddlers.

In chapter 4, James describes the person who is in love with the things of this world as an adulterer. He is like a married man who expects to enjoy all the fruits of a happy marriage while flaunting his dalliance with girlfriends. It doesn't work. Chasing after the world is as damaging to friendship with God as adultery is to marriage. The two cannot co-exist.

So, is there a solution? Yes, of course! James offers the same counsel as the prophet who confronted Amaziah:

> *"Submit yourselves, then, to God. Resist the devil, and he will flee from you. Come near to God and he will come near to you. Wash your hands, you sinners, and purify your hearts, you double-minded. Grieve, mourn, and wail. Change your laughter to mourning and your joy to gloom. Humble yourselves before the Lord, and he will lift you up."*
>
> James 4:7-10

The besetting sin of our Western culture is not rebellion against God, but double-mindedness. The people who call themselves Christians know enough to acknowledge the superiority of Christian values, but their hearts are not fully committed to Christ. They have a divided loyalty between the kingdom of God and the things of this world. Their desire for worldly approval keeps them from enjoying the abundance of a life fully devoted to God. As James warned, they ask of God, but don't receive. How sad!

The revival for which we pray is not so much that flagrant sinners would denounce their wickedness, but that nice people would repent of their double-minded adultery with the world.

# CHAPTER 7

# Uzziah: The King with an Arrogant Heart

Arrogate (ar'ro-gate): "to grasp, claim, or assume powers, position, privileges, or prestige which have not been properly granted, earned, or bestowed."

An arrogant person is someone who places himself or herself in an unauthorized role. In England, the height of arrogance is to call oneself "Sir-Something-or-Other" without being officially knighted. In organizations, an arrogant person is the one who acts like the boss without being assigned, appointed, or elected to that position. In ancient Judah, King Uzziah was a fine leader until he usurped the role of the high priest and entered the Holy of Holies to offer sacrifices. His arrogance offended God, and it cost him dearly.

Otherwise, Uzziah was a wonderful king. He ruled for 52 years and brought prosperity, peace, and spiritual health to the nation of Judah. Like his father Amaziah, "he did what was right in the eyes of the Lord."

> *"He sought God during the days of Zechariah, who instructed him in the fear of God. As long as he sought the Lord, God gave him success."*          II Chronicles 26:5

However, near the end of his successful reign, an insidious temptation crept into Uzziah's heart: the desire to officiate as high priest for the nation of Judah as well as to rule as king. God had decreed that the rituals of the temple must be conducted exclusively by priests from the family of Levi, including the office of the high priest. Only the high priest could offer sacrifices on the Golden Altar, and the people of Judah had always followed those instructions. However, up in the northern kingdom of Israel, the idolatrous King Jeroboam had appointed himself not only king, but high priest as well. Perhaps Uzziah thought, "If Jeroboam can have both positions, why can't I?" Bad thinking!

The story of Uzziah's downfall follows a familiar pattern—a pattern often repeated in the Books of Chronicles: The king was tempted by pride, pride led to an overt act of defiance of God's law, God sent messengers to warn the king, the king ignored the messengers and did what he wanted, and God struck him down. In Uzziah's case, he entered the sacred temple with the intention of offering sacrifices. The high priest, Ahaziah, and eighty other priests tried to prevent him. When he lifted the scepter of incense as though he were the high priest, he was stricken with leprosy on his forehead. Uzziah was so mortified, he ran from the temple in disgrace. Because leprosy was such a dreaded disease, Uzziah was forced to live in a remote house away from the rest of the people. Although he was still officially the king, his son ran the nation of Judah in his place. Even when he died, he was not allowed to be buried in the cemetery with the other great kings, but was buried separately.

People often confuse "pride" and "arrogance." They are not the same. Pride is an attitude; arrogance is an action. Pride is the root; arrogance is the fruit. Pride is a puffed-up opinion of oneself; arrogance is usurping a position or privilege which has not been granted. Pride is a disposition of the heart which can either remain hidden or can be overtly expressed as an arrogant action.

God, by the convicting work of the Holy Spirit, will correct pride—hopefully before it is expressed in arrogant behavior. Pride triggers God's patient, but persistent, discipline. Arrogance, on the other hand, provokes God's immediate wrath. He will not tolerate it.

According to our traditional theology, Satan was an angel overcome by arrogance. He tried to usurp the authority of God, and it led to his expulsion from heaven.

Adam, our first ancestor, was tempted by Satan to arrogate to himself the right to make his own rules. When he ate of the forbidden tree of the knowledge of good and evil, his sin was not merely disobedience: it was arrogance. He was saying, "I'll decide what I can do and not do. I'll make the rules." His problem was not just pride—an elevated opinion of himself. God will discipline one of his children who succumbs to pride. But Adam's offense was far more serious than pride.

Uzziah would have been forgotten except for a casual reference to his death in the prophecy of Isaiah:

> *"In the year that King Uzziah died, I saw the Lord, high and lifted up..."* Isaiah 6:1

Because of his humility in the presence of God, Isaiah's vision of The Almighty has been forever etched in the minds of God's people. His name is attached to one of the most-quoted descriptions of the awesome majesty of God in all of human history. Because of his arrogance, the name of Uzziah is merely a historical bookmark, linking God's revelation of Himself to Isaiah to a time and place in Judah's history.

Nobody remembers the name of those who shake their fists in the face of God. Who can remember the names of any of the world's great atheists? Or who can list the accomplishments of anyone who was motivated to great humanitarian contributions by their contempt for God? However, our bookshelves are full of biographies of people who did great exploits fueled by their high and holy view of God.

So, how does one begin to gain an awareness of God's greatness and avoid the arrogance which so displeases Him?

A good place to start is with a physical act of submission to God's authority. When a commanding officer walks into a room, what do the soldiers do? They stand at attention and salute. When the judge enters the courtroom, what does everyone in the courtroom do? They stand until the judge gives them permission to be seated. When God confronted Moses at the burning bush, what did Moses do? He took off his shoes, acknowledging God's holiness. When Thomas met the risen Christ, what did he do? He fell on his knees and declared, "My Lord and my God!"

What is the significance of these acts of submission? They acknowledge and affirm that the person to whom they are submitting has the right, the authority, and the power to establish the rules. Those in his presence have the obligation (or privilege) of abiding by his decisions and carrying out his commands.

So what must we—we who would experience the greatness of God—what must we do to enter his presence? We must begin with a physical demonstration of our submission to his authority: kneel, fall prostrate on our faces, bow our heads, come forward to an altar of commitment, undergo water baptism—whatever it takes to abandon the right to be in control. How often should we practice these gestures? Daily at best, as often as necessary to relinquish any scrap of independence.

Then what? Following Isaiah's example, we declare our total inability to deserve an audience with God:

> *"Woe to me!' I cried. 'I am ruined! For I am a man of unclean lips, and I live among a people of unclean lips, and my eyes have seen the King, the Lord Almighty.'"*
>
> Isaiah 6:5

If our motivation is pure and our response to God's presence is genuine, he will say to us, just as he said to Isaiah,

> *"Whom shall I send? And who will go for us?"*
>
> Isaiah 6:8

God has a unique mission for everyone who submits to his authority. None of us receives the same assignment, but we all march to the orders of the same commander. Our encounter with the overwhelming presence of the King propels us into productive service for his kingdom. With genuine humility we respond, in the words of Isaiah:

> *"Here am I. Send me!"*

In his first letter to the Church, the Apostle Peter used an intriguing word to describe humility—a word used only once in the New Testament. In I Peter 5:5 he says,

> *"All of you, **clothe** yourselves with humility toward one another, because 'God opposes the proud but gives grace to the humble.'"*

The J.B. Phillips translation renders the word *enkombousthai* as "put on the overalls" of humility. This word refers to the kind of leather apron a blacksmith would wear. In our day, Peter might have used "the white uniform a nurse wears," or "the coveralls of a mechanic," or "the blue scrubs a surgeon wears." The picture Peter paints of true humility is not self-deprecation or speaking poorly of oneself. Rather, humility is accepting the job we've been assigned and dressing accordingly.

Jesus, of course, is our model. As Paul wrote to the Philippians,

> *"Your attitude should be the same as that of Christ Jesus: Who, being in very nature God, did not consider equality with God something to be grasped, but made himself nothing, taking the very nature of a servant, being made in human likeness. And being found in appearance as a man, he humbled himself and became obedient to death—even death on a cross! Therefore God exalted him to the highest place and gave him the name that is above every name, that at the name of Jesus every knee should bow, in heaven and on earth and under the earth, and every tongue confess that Jesus Christ is Lord, to the glory of God the Father."*
>
> Philippians 2:5-11

Jesus did not abrogate his rightful role as God; rather, he voluntarily laid it aside for a season in order to accomplish his God-given mission.

What a contrast: Uzziah, the little king of Judah, who tried to take over God's holy temple, and Jesus, the eternal

Son of God, who left the glory of heaven to suffer and die for us. Uzziah was buried in the shame of failure in a leper's tomb; Jesus left the tomb to rise in the glory of a victorious completion of the Father's mission. May we learn from the outcome of Uzziah's arrogance to seek the Lord's face, to humble ourselves in his presence, to confess our emptiness before him, and to accept his assignment, wherever that may lead.

CHAPTER 8

# Hezekiah: The Power of an Undivided Heart

*"Teach me your way, O Lord, and I will walk in your truth; give me an undivided heart, that I may fear your name."* Psalm 86:11

Hezekiah was a great king and a great man. His life demonstrates what God can do through a person who has an undivided heart toward him. He became king of Judah when he was 25 years of age and ruled in Jerusalem for 29 years.

*"Hezekiah trusted in the Lord, the God of Israel. There was no one like him among all the kings of Judah, either before him or after him. He held fast to the Lord and did not cease to follow him; he kept the commands the Lord*

*had given to Moses. And the Lord was with him; he was successful in whatever he undertook."*

II Kings 18:5-7

Who wouldn't want that etched into his tombstone: "He was successful in whatever he undertook?" Let's look at some of the things he accomplished, then examine the secret of his success:

1. The very first thing he did after he was crowned king ("in the first month of the first year of his reign" (II Chronicles 29:3)) was to restore the nation's relationship with God. He started with cleansing the temple. Not only did he throw out everything that was impure or unholy; he got rid of everything that was even questionable. One of the relics which had been kept in the temple was the bronze serpent which had been Israel's means of deliverance during their wandering in the wilderness. However, over the years it had become an object of veneration and the people had been burning incense to it. So, he broke it into pieces! Not even the means of salvation would be allowed to distract people from a complete and wholehearted devotion to God alone.

He explained to all the spiritual leaders (priests and Levites) the reason for cleansing the temple and restoring proper worship:

*"Our fathers were unfaithful; they did evil in the eyes of the Lord our God and forsook him. They turned their faces*

*away from the Lord's dwelling place and turned their backs on him...Therefore, the anger of the Lord has fallen on Judah and Jerusalem; he has made them an object of dread and horror and scorn, as you can see with your own eyes."*

II Chronicles 29:6-8

As is true with every great revival of religion, Hezekiah's reform started with repentance. He made no excuses for the deplorable state of Judah's condition, other than to acknowledge that God had been true to his warning: "If you forsake me, I will forsake you."

Building on the foundation of that contrite and humble confession, he declared that the whole nation must renew their covenant with God. Remember: a "covenant" is a verbal expression of a heartfelt commitment of love and loyalty, symbolized by the ritual shedding of blood, the offering of sacrificial gifts, and the sharing of a common meal. The highlight of the covenant ceremony was the restoration of the Feast of the Passover, which had not been properly observed for many generations. The Passover was a ritual reenactment of God's deliverance of his people from slavery in Egypt and symbolic of his personal forgiveness for the sins of the people. Everyone brought a sacrificial lamb, whose shed blood was the requirement for forgiveness of sins against God.

*"Hezekiah gave the order to sacrifice the burnt offering on the altar. As the offering began, singing to the Lord began also, accompanied by trumpets and the instruments of David king of Israel. The whole assembly bowed in*

*worship, while the singers sang and the trumpeters played. All this continued until the sacrifice of the burnt offering was completed. When the offerings were finished, the king and everyone present with him knelt down and worshiped."*
II Chronicles 29:27-29

This was a jubilant celebration, including all the elements of spiritual revival: confession, repentance, cleansing, prayer, praise, worship, and restoration of a covenant fellowship with God. Even Hezekiah was amazed that it could be done so quickly. (II Chronicles 29:36)

2. Hezekiah's reign over the kingdom of Judah coincided with the rise of one of the great ancient empires: the Assyrians. Under the leadership of the King Shalmaneser, the Assyrian armies swept through the Middle East, gobbling up one nation after another. One of his successors, King Sennacherib, launched a siege against Samaria, the capital of the northern kingdom of Israel, and subdued it three years later. The ten tribes of Israel were deported into various parts of the Assyrian empire, never to be heard from again. Then, Sennacherib turned his forces on Judah. They captured a number of Judean towns, carried off all their wealth, and took hundreds of thousands of captives. Hezekiah paid the Assyrians the duty they demanded of him, but he refused to give up the city of Jerusalem.

In 701 B.C., Sennacherib began march on Jerusalem with a great army. He sent a taunting message to Hezekiah, then to all the people of Jerusalem:

*"Do not let Hezekiah mislead you when he says, 'The Lord will deliver us.' Has the god of any nation ever delivered his land from the hand of the king of Assyria? Where are the gods of Hamath and Arpad? Where are the gods of Sepharvaim? Have they rescued Samaria from my hand? Who of all the gods of these countries has been able to save his land from me? How then can the Lord deliver Jerusalem from my hand?"* Isaiah 36:18-20

Hezekiah humbled himself before the Lord and went to the temple to pray. He sent his administrators to inform the prophet Isaiah to seek the Lord's solution to this terrible situation. In the temple, he spread out the letter of Sennacherib before the Lord and prayed this prayer:

*"O Lord Almighty, God of Israel, enthroned between the cherubim, you alone are God over all the kingdoms of the earth. You have made heaven and earth. Give ear, O Lord, and hear; open your eyes, O Lord, and see; listen to all the words Sennacherib has sent to insult the living God. It is true, O Lord, that the Assyrian kings have laid waste all these peoples and their lands. They have thrown their gods into the fire and destroyed them, for they were not gods but only wood and stone, fashioned by human hands. Now, O Lord our God, deliver us from his hand, so that all kingdoms on earth may know that you alone, O Lord, are God."* Isaiah 37:16-20

That night, the angel of the Lord struck the armies of the Assyrians. In the morning, when the people of Jerusalem went out to the camp of the Assyrians, they found 185,000 bodies. Sennacherib had retreated in disgrace. When he returned to Nineveh, he was assassinated by his own sons while he was worshipping in the temple of his god.

3. Hezekiah also left a legacy of practical improvements in the city of Jerusalem. One of the most enduring legacies was the aqueduct he built from the spring of Gihon to a cistern on the west side of the city. This greatly reduced Jerusalem's vulnerability to foreign invaders by denying water to attackers and providing a dependable water supply within the city walls. This tunnel, cut through solid rock, was 1,700 feet long and from nearly four feet to nearly 12 feet in height.

The secret of Hezekiah's success was his absolute trust in the Lord his God. His loyalty to God never wavered, and he never compromised his commitment to God. At one point in his life, he was convinced he was going to die. He had a serious infection which threatened his life. He inquired of Isaiah, the prophet, who told him:

> *"Put your house in order, because you are going to die; you will not recover."*                                    II Kings 20:1

However, Hezekiah appealed to the one quality which the Lord would honor: an undivided heart. He wept bitterly and cried out to God,

> *"Remember, O Lord, how I have walked before you faithfully and with wholehearted devotion and have done what is good in your eyes."*                          II Kings 20:3

The Lord responded in mercy and promised him an additional fifteen years of life. He gave him a miraculous sign, moving the shadow of the sun backwards then forward again, that he would carry out what he had promised.

Now, it must be noted that the record of Hezekiah is not without blemish. In at least one instance, Hezekiah offended the God he loved. As he prospered and grew wealthy, pride crept into his heart. Envoys from the king of Babylon had heard of his illness and miraculous recovery, and they came to pay him a visit. In his eagerness to display his own accomplishments, Hezekiah showed off all the treasures he had accumulated. He led them through his palace and storehouses and showed them all his gold, silver, oils, spices, and armaments.

True to his role as God's messenger, the prophet Isaiah confronted him:

> "What did those men say, and where did they come from?"

> "From a distant land," Hezekiah replied. "They came from Babylon."

> The prophet asked, "What did they see in your palace?"

> "They saw everything in my palace," Hezekiah said. "There is nothing among my treasures that I did not show them."

Then Isaiah said to Hezekiah, *"Hear the word of the Lord: The time will surely come when everything in your palace, and all that your fathers have stored up until this day, will be carried off to Babylon. Nothing will be left, says the Lord. And some of your descendants, your own flesh and blood, that will be born to you, will be taken away, and they will become eunuchs in the palace of the king of Babylon."*                                   II Kings 20:14-18

When he realized how his pride had offended God, Hezekiah repented and the Lord's wrath was averted. He was restored to his fellowship with God.

This incident raises an important question: Is it possible for a person who has an undivided heart toward God to sin against God and rouse his anger? And, if such occurs, what can be done? Is an undivided heart something that, once lost, can never be regained?

The accounts of God's dealings with all the kings of Judah, including David and Hezekiah, give a clear message: Sometimes God's most devoted people do things that offend him. He will not hold back his anger simply because they are his children or even because they have followed him faithfully in the past. However, in every case, the Lord offers both a warning and a path to restoration. He requires confession, repentance, and restitution. He will restore his children to their former relationship, but the consequences of their wrong behavior may still be felt.

The Apostle Paul addresses this problem in his first letter to the Corinthian church, chapter 11. Right in the middle of his directions about how to observe the Lord's Supper, he gives this instruction:

> *"But if we judged ourselves, we would not come under judgment. When we are judged by the Lord, we are being disciplined so that we will not be condemned with the world."*
>
> I Corinthians 11:31-32

We who are God's children should constantly evaluate our own words, actions, and thoughts. When we sense that we have erred or even started in a wrong direction, we should "judge ourselves" and ask for grace to get back on track. If we have done or said something we know to be wrong, we should immediately confess and repent. We need to keep short accounts with God. If we do not judge ourselves, God will judge us unto correction, just as a loving father disciplines his child. If we respond to God's correction, he will forgive us and restore us to his favor. However, if we insist on provoking God's anger, we will be more and more severely chastened.

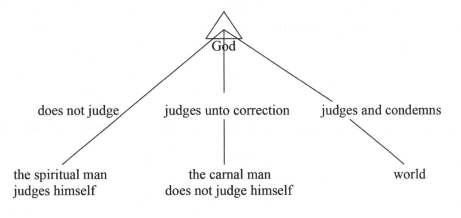

It is significant that this passage on "judging ourselves" comes in the middle of the service of the Lord's Supper. Evaluating our own behavior is difficult; it is hard to be ruthlessly honest about our actions, much less the "thoughts and intentions of our hearts." However, as we hold in our hands the reminders of Jesus' shed blood and broken body, being reminded again of his sacrifice for us and his covenant love for us, we are on much firmer ground in dealing with our own errors.

Despite the fact that God had to deal severely with Hezekiah about his pride, he still is a great model for us today. He demonstrated the power of heart-felt devotion. He illustrated what God's people should do when they are convicted of pride—or other sins. And he presented us a model for personal success.

Success: that's a hot topic these days. Whole shelves in the self-help section of every bookstore purport to tell people how to succeed. Each author has his or her own formula for accomplishing great things. However, I have never read about Hezekiah in any of those books, nor have I ever heard of one which advocated the secret of success Hezekiah discovered: the power of an undivided heart.

# CHAPTER 9

# Josiah: The Man Who Trembles at God's Word

*"This is the one I esteem: he who is humble and contrite in spirit, and trembles at my word."*          Isaiah 66:2

Josiah was a king who got God's attention—his favorable attention. He was one of the last kings of Judah. His father Amon and his grandfather Manasseh were ungodly kings who worshipped false gods and led Judah into abominable practices. But Josiah turned things around. He made an amazing discovery which enabled him to lead his people to revival and reform—a discovery which is available to anyone who seeks to have an undivided heart toward God.

After his father's death, Josiah was crowned king. He was only eight years old at the time, but already he was on the right path:

> *"He did what was right in the eyes of the Lord and walked in the ways of his father David, not turning aside to the right or the left."* II Chronicles 34:2

The chronicler gives us a time line, not only of Josiah's actions as king, but of the stages of his spiritual development. We can't read too much into what Josiah did at each level of his growth, but it does provide a useful yardstick to measure a person's progress.

When our three children were small, we frequently checked their progress against accepted norms. At twelve months, most kids have learned to walk. One of ours walked at eight months, the other two later, so there was a range considered "normal." We weren't concerned about their progress as long as they were somewhere in "normal" range. However, if one of our children had failed to walk by three or four years of age, that would have been cause for serious concern. We would have needed to take remedial action.

There are similar growth patterns in a person's spiritual life. Josiah's spiritual growth chart is not necessarily the norm, but it does provide points for discussion about what a person should be doing at each stage of spiritual maturity.

We learn from the chronicler that by the time he took office at **eight years of age:**

*"He did what was right in the eyes of the Lord and walked in the ways of his father David, not turning aside to the right or to the left."* II Chronicles 34:2

This description reveals two interrelated aspects of Josiah's character: First, he knew right from wrong, and he determined to do what was right—with no exceptions. This may not apply in all situations, but by eight years of age a child should have a clear understanding of what is right and wrong and a settled disposition to choose what is right. If not, he/she needs serious remedial attention.

We're not told exactly how Josiah learned right from wrong. He certainly didn't learn it from his father. We do know the name of his mother and her lineage. Perhaps, despite his father's poor example, his mother instilled in his heart not only a clear set of values, but a heart-felt desire to choose what is right.

One thing we learned early in our children's development: Don't ask, "Why did you do that?" when they willfully disobeyed. That's just training a child to be an excuse-maker at best and a liar at worst. The question should be, "Was what you did the right thing or the wrong thing? What should you have done?" The goal is to train a child's conscience so that the standard of right and wrong is always the measuring stick. Nor should a parent appeal to the child's feelings: "You hurt my feelings by doing that!" No, a child isn't responsible for his parents' feelings; he is responsible to do what is right. The child must learn to *want* what is right.

If a four-year-old does something that displays poor judgment, not a violation of clearly-understood rules of conduct, this is an opportunity for instruction, not discipline. However, if his/her actions display a deliberate flouting of standards of right and wrong, correction is in order. The goal is to instill in a child's heart a life-long set of moral standards and a joy in choosing the right way. Apparently, Josiah learned this at an early age.

Secondly, Josiah was aware of the great spiritual legacy that had as its model the great King David, handed down through generations of David's descendents. Josiah knew he was the bearer of a godly heritage, and he was determined to live up to that standard. Perhaps the priest Hilkiah schooled him in David's history. If a family has a godly heritage, it is a wise investment to keep that heritage fresh in every child's mind through stories, pictures, traditions, and extended-family gatherings.

When Josiah was **sixteen years of age** ("the eighth year of his reign"), he entered a new stage of his personal development:

> *"In the eighth year of his reign, while he was still young, he began to seek the God of his father David."*
>
> II Chronicles 34:3

Seeking God: that's a wise and noble quest for a teenager. Just as his ancestor David had sought to know God when he was a teenager tending his father's sheep, so Josiah set his heart on the same quest. The teen years

are the ideal time to make a personal effort to know
God. Younger children learn the values and beliefs of
their parents, but teenagers are in the process of forging
their own belief systems, moving from the faith of their
parents to their own personal relationship with God. For
some, this is an easy process: it is hard to say when the
transition actually takes place. For others, it is a tough
struggle. The important issue is not how it takes place,
but that it happens. Wise parents will not only recognize
that a child needs to cut the ties of dependency on them,
but to encourage an independent pursuit of their own
knowledge of God's reality.

When I was about twelve or thirteen, our church was
preparing to host a series of meetings with the great
Indian evangelist, Sam Kamalesan. The elders of our
church were gathered in my father's study to welcome him.
I stood in the doorway, not wanting to miss whatever was
going on. I'll never forget that occasion: Dr. Kamalesan
greeted all the adults in the room, then came directly to
me and asked, "What is the Lord doing in your life?" Me?
I wasn't aware that the Lord should be doing anything
in my life. I only knew I was to be seen and not heard.
But his question (and subsequent discussions) helped me
realize it was time to do some serious thinking about my
own place in God's kingdom.

The teen years are the appropriate time to dig deep wells
of spiritual commitment. Of course, it is possible for
people to come to a personal friendship with God at
any stage of life, but it is healthiest to drive down those

personal stakes early, when the heart is pliable and the ruts of habit are not too deep to change.

At **age twenty** ("the twelfth year of his reign"), young King Josiah set out on the next phase of his spiritual pilgrimage: the work of God. He tackled two main projects: ridding the nation of all traces of idolatry and repairing the temple in Jerusalem. For more than 70 years, the people of Judah had suffered the corrupting consequences of worshipping pagan gods. There were altars and "high places" and centers of idol worship throughout the country. Instead of looking to God's prophets and priests for guidance, the people turned to mediums, soothsayers, and witches. Manasseh, Josiah's grandfather, had even offered some of his children as burnt sacrifices to these pagan gods. The morality of the people followed the character of their gods: perverted, cruel, and capricious.

Josiah knew this was wrong. He set about cleansing the nation of every trace of idol worship. He tore down the altars and "high places." He burned the wooden images, ground them into dust, and sprinkled the ashes on the graves of those who had worshipped them. He even dug up the bones of the pagan priests and burned them on the altars they had built.

Every revival of religion entails a clear break with false religion, whatever the prevailing "idolatry" may be. The great East Africa Revival began in Rwanda in 1929 and spread throughout that whole region: Tanzania,

Kenya, Uganda, and Burundi. People came under great conviction about their false religions and burned their fetishes, their idols, their magic charms. The cleansing of those areas had a profound effect on communities all throughout east Africa, and its impact continues to be felt to this day. Those areas of southern Africa not touched by the revival continue to have problems with syncretism: people accepting Christianity on the surface but clinging to their fetishes and charms "just in case."

The Mormons have this much right: twenty is the optimal age for immersion into the work of the church. Their teenagers get several years of "seminary" training in conjunction with high school in preparation for two years of missionary service—at their parents' expense. This is considered the "norm" of spiritual growth among Mormon families. Whatever flaws the Mormons may have in their doctrine, this practice is right.

I recently sat on a plane next to a young man returning from two years of Mormon missionary service in Brazil. He eagerly shared with me the lessons he had learned from working in the slums of a large city under the supervision of church mentors. He attempted to persuade me, a total stranger, to commit myself to a life of personal holiness, of spiritual discipline, and of sacrificial giving!

The evangelical church, on the other hand, is losing its "twenty-somethings." In a desperate attempt to reach them, the church has brought in flashy entertainment, loud music, and cute programs. The effort is failing: some "twenty-somethings" quietly slip away, others flee the church like their hair is on fire. It's the wrong approach. What this younger generation wants is an opportunity to get their hands dirty righting the wrongs of their world. They want significant involvement in work that makes a real difference. They want immersion in the transformation of the world.

Jesus modeled this strategy with his disciples. As soon as their commitment to follow him was solid, he took them on mission trips. He led them through the towns and villages of Judea, into the cross-cultural environment of Samaria, and into the city of Jerusalem. What were they doing? They were doing good: healing the sick, casting out demons, and announcing that God's kingdom was at hand. Compassionate service was the context in which Jesus made disciples. It was the classroom in which he trained them in the principles of the Kingdom.

At the outset of his ministry, Jesus stood up to read the scripture in the synagogue in his home town of Nazareth. Surely his disciples were with him when he announced his mission, based on the prophecy of Isaiah:

> *"The Spirit of the Lord is on me, because he has anointed me to preach good news to the poor. He has sent me to proclaim freedom for the prisoners and recovery of sight for the blind, to release the oppressed, to proclaim the year of the Lord's favor."*                    Luke 4:18-19

The religious leaders of Nazareth were furious, but apparently his friends said, "We could get into that! Let's follow him." They did follow him, and he led them on a journey to fulfill that mission he had just announced.

Josiah's other project was rebuilding the temple, the place of worship. He brought in masons and carpenters and workers to repair the damage done by seventy years of desecration. In the course of working on God's house, he found the opportunity to move up to the next level of spiritual growth.

When Josiah was **26 years old** ("the 18th year of his reign"), he made a life-changing discovery: the Word of God. Hilkiah the priest discovered the long-lost Books of Moses, which we call the Pentateuch—the first five books of the Old Testament. How it had survived the neglect and abuse of the temple under the ungodly kings before Josiah (like Amon and Manassah) we don't know. What we do know is that God preserved it, Hilkiah discovered it, and Josiah read it.

Josiah's first response was terror. He knew this scroll contained the Law of the Lord, but he didn't know how to deal with the judgment it promised:

> *"Great is the Lord's anger that is poured out on us because our fathers have not kept the word of the Lord; they have not acted in accordance with all that is written in this book."*
> II Chronicles 34:21

His second response, and a good one, was to find a godly person who could interpret the meaning of the Scripture to him. Hilkiah went to Huldah, a prophetess, and asked her to "inquire of the Lord" about the coming calamity. Although anyone can glean truth from God's Word on his own (or hers), it is always helpful to have a guide, a tutor, a mentor. As one of my African colleagues says, "The Bible is like a great forest: if you enter there without a guide, you can become lost or discouraged."

The next step was personal commitment to obey the requirements of the Book.

> *"The king stood by his pillar and renewed the covenant in the presence of the Lord—to follow the Lord and keep his commands, regulations and decrees with all his heart and all his soul, and to obey the words of the covenant written in this book."* II Chronicles 34:31

Then he encouraged all this people to do the same. Actually, he made them do it, but they did so gladly following the example of their beloved king.

> *"As long as he lived, they did not fail to follow the Lord, the God of their fathers."* II Chronicles 34:33b

The final stage of Josiah's renewal was restoration of the Passover celebration. This feast commemorated Israel's deliverance from bondage in Egypt. It was a sensory reminder to God's people, "You were once slaves; now, by God's saving grace, you are free."

Jesus celebrated this same feast with his disciples, giving new meaning to the ancient celebration. He instituted a new feast, the Lord's Supper, which is a constant reminder of the covenant bond between himself and those whose hearts are undivided toward him.

Two great forces combined to make Josiah a mighty man: his desire to seek and serve God and God's revelation through his written Word. Because of his desire to apply God's Word to every aspect of his life, Josiah gained God's blessing and brought renewal to his nation. What finer epitaph could be given to anyone than this:

> *"Neither before nor after Josiah was there a king like him who turned to the Lord as he did—with all his heart and with all his soul and with all his strength, in accordance with all the Law of Moses."*      II Kings 23:25

# Why Study the Kings of Judah?

Many people fail to discover the value of studying the Old Testament. They get bogged down in the genealogies, the dietary restrictions, the unpronounceable names, or the graphic descriptions of warfare as it was carried out 3,000 years ago. In frustration, they may turn to scholarly commentaries and become even more confused. Many of the reference books were written by technical linguistic scholars for other professional scholars, and their endless squabbles over who wrote what may leave the average reader unsatisfied.

It is legitimate and reasonable for a reader to ask, "Do these commentators share my same reverence for God's Word, or are they just literary specialists who approach the scriptures with the same detachment as biologists studying a laboratory specimen? Has this scholar had the same kind of personal encounter with Christ as I have, and does he or she really believe these writings to be the Word of God?" Those are legitimate concerns.

Another set of questions is also relevant: "Has this commentator ever worked in a local church, helping people grow spiritually and dealing with the everyday issues of Christian living? Does he or she interpret the scriptures in light of their application to practical and problematic human issues? Are their interpretations of the Bible written for people who are eagerly looking to God's Word for inspiration and instruction?"

I have found one commentator on the Old Testament whom I personally trust. I recommend him to anyone who wants to glean useful information from those ancient scriptures. He studied with the greatest Jewish scholars of his day, and he lived his life in strict compliance with the guidelines laid down in the Torah, the books of Moses. He had a personal encounter with Jesus Christ, and from that moment onward he served Christ's church in several countries of the world. Most importantly for me, he spent his time every day proclaiming the good news of Christ's resurrection and helping those who accepted that gospel to grow spiritually.

His name is Paul, formerly Saul of Tarsus. He studied under Gamaliel, the greatest biblical scholar of his day—right in Jerusalem, where many of the events of the Old

Testament took place. He met Jesus in a dramatic encounter on the road to Damascus, and he was transformed from a persecutor of Christians into a faithful servant of Christ. He accepted the commission to take the message of Christ to the non-Jewish world beyond the borders of Palestine, and he established churches throughout several parts of the Roman Empire. Throughout his ministry, he used the Old Testament scriptures as an effective tool to train disciples in the ways of God.

Here's what Paul had to say about the value of studying the Old Testament:

To his young apprentice Timothy he wrote:

> *"All Scripture is God-breathed and is useful for teaching, rebuking, correcting and training in righteousness, so that the man of God may be thoroughly equipped for every good work."*     II Timothy 3:16-17

The "Scripture" Paul is referring to is the Old Testament. It was the Bible of the early church. Paul assures his young colleague that the collection of writings that had been handed down through the Jewish community were indeed inspired by God. Their practical value is not only that they are the anchor, the foundation, of a belief system (teaching), but they are powerful tools for guiding human behavior (rebuking, correcting, training in righteousness).

Theologians may quibble over the definition of "righteousness," but at least in the Bible of Jesus' day, righteousness meant "doing the right thing in the right way for the right reasons." And what is the standard of "right-ness?" The Bible—as first revealed to the prophets, patriarchs, and priests who penned the Old Testament by inspiration of God.

One of the churches Paul established in what is now Europe was the group of believers at Corinth. They had not grown up with an understanding of God's revelation to the Jews; they grew up in a pagan culture. The only religion their families had ever known was rooted in pagan myths, animistic fables, and the worship of the natural world as represented by carved figurines—idols. Paul introduced the stories of the kings of Judah, along with the other revealed Old Testament writings, as an instructional manual on how to live out their new life in Christ. Here's what he told them:

> *"Now these things occurred as examples to keep us from setting our hearts on evil things as they did. Do not be idolaters, as some of them were; as it is written: "The people sat down to eat and drink and got up to indulge in pagan revelry." We should not commit sexual immorality, as some of them did—and in one day twenty-three thousand of them died. We should not test the Lord, as some of them did—and were killed by snakes. And do not grumble, as some of them did—and were killed by the destroying angel."*                    I Corinthians 10:6-10

What better instruction could these new converts from paganism have than the tragic stories of Joash, Manassah, etc? They could trace the tragic consequences of idol worship through several generations of the family of David. And what better warning against sexual misconduct could they receive than hearing what happened to David or Solomon? Paul even told them that studying those examples could help them avoid demanding that God give them signs ("testing God") or grumbling even when God was providing for all their needs. (See Psalm 95 and Hebrews 3 for an explanation of why complaining is so displeasing to God.)

To his friends in Rome, Paul gave this hopeful advice:

> *"For everything that was written in the past was written to teach us, so that through endurance and the encouragement of the Scriptures we might have hope."*
>
> Romans 15:4

To be a follower of Jesus in the Roman Empire in those early days of the church was a daunting task. It was not easy for those first-century Christians to remain firm in their faith when members of their fellowship were being thrown to the lions in the arena or burned at the stake. How could they persevere, how could they maintain a positive outlook, how could they keep from quitting, when the powers of the empire were stacked against them? By holding to "everything that was written in the past," by reading again and again the accounts of God's faithfulness to those who had an undivided heart.

Do we still live in a culture absorbed with "pagan revelry," as Paul described the world in which the Corinthians lived?

Are we bombarded every day with images, music, and suggestive advertising which seek to lure us into sexual immorality? Are we tempted by an unfriendly culture to lose hope and quit? How shall we prevail? Where can we find solid ground on which to stand? One good place to start is by reading again the life stories of the kings of Judah. The promise of God is as true today as it was in the days of Asa when the prophet told him:

> *"The eyes of the Lord run to and fro throughout the whole earth, to show himself strong on behalf of those whose hearts are undivided toward him."*
>
> II Chronicles 16:9 KJV

# Rafiki Books

is a subsidiary of Heart of Africa, Inc.
Rafiki is the Swahili word for "friends."
The purpose of these publications
is to help our friends
help their friends
follow Jesus Christ,
doing the kinds of things in their world
which he did in his.

Heart of Africa is a mission
whose purpose is to help our African colleagues
fulfill their God-given ministries.
It is a 501(c)(3) organization.

Learn more at:
www.heartofafrica.org
and www.rafikibooks.com

Contact:
Rafiki Books
P.O. Box 5
Wilmore, Kentucky 40390
MHAfrica@aol.com
407-619-3482

Made in the USA
Middletown, DE
27 October 2020